The Minor Prophets

THE COMPLETE PORTRAIT
OF THE MESSIAH

Volume 9

Other volumes in The Complete Portrait of the Messiah series

Also available from Time to Revive and Laura Kim Martin

reviveDAILY: A Devotional Journey from Genesis to Revelation, Year 1
reviveDAILY: A Devotional Journey from Genesis to Revelation, Year 2

The Minor Prophets

THE COMPLETE PORTRAIT
OF THE MESSIAH

Volume 9

Kyle Lance Martin

Time to Revive and reviveSCHOOL

time to
revive
Richardson, Texas

The Minor Prophets

Published in conjunction with
Iron Stream Media
100 Missionary Ridge
Birmingham, AL 35242
IronStreamMedia.com

Library of Congress Control Number: 2024907566

978-1-63204-111-1 (hardback)
978-1-63204-112-8 (eBook)

1 2 3 4 5—28 27 26 25 24

DEDICATION

Greetings friends and colaborers of the Lord Jesus Christ!

I am writing to you with an excitement that is beyond words. For I would like to dedicate this book to individuals like yourselves whose desire to grow closer to Jesus and go deeper in the Word of God brings such JOY to my heart. And my prayer for each one of you is that the Holy Spirit will reveal more of Himself to you in this in-depth time of studying the Word of God daily. Jesus said, "Blessed are those who hunger and thirst for righteousness, for they will be satisfied" (Matthew 5:6 NASB). So as you embark on this journey of studying each book of the Bible, may you experience a freshness and a fulfillment that can only come from the Spirit of God. You will have days that you won't want to wake up early and read. There will be moments when life throws you a situation that delays your personal devotional time with Him. But please press in and allow the Holy Spirit to strengthen your every step. This will allow you to exercise your faith muscles and walk out what you are learning in this. From my experience, obedience will bring education to life!

It will be quite a strenuous commitment, yet it's a part of an intentional strategy to equip the saints for His return. And your participation with reviveSCHOOL is a unique part of this preparation.

May the Lord receive all the glory, honor, and fame in this pursuit of righteousness.

Praying,
Dr. Kyle Lance Martin

CONTENTS

reviveSCHOOL History and Introduction

In January of 2015, our ministry, Time to Revive, was invited from our home base in Richardson, Texas, to Goshen, Indiana, to help equip the local church to learn how to go out and share the gospel in their community. We called it reviveINDIANA. During this frigid first trip in January, our intention was to help facilitate a week of prayer and outreach as a form of training, which we hoped would lead to an intentional week of outreach later that year. Little did we know that God had other plans.

The week of prayer and outreach started with about 450 people from various churches in the community and, to our surprise, quickly swelled to over 3,000. And by the end of that first week, the Holy Spirit confirmed to a group of us, including local pastors, that the Time to Revive team should stay for 52 straight days! Imagine the phone calls we had to make to our spouses telling them we were going to stay a "little" longer.

Over the course of these seven weeks, the local church witnessed God move in mighty ways, and each person involved could tell you miraculous testimonies of how they witnessed, firsthand, how God was moving. The 52 days culminated on March 4 of that year where an estimated 10,000 people showed up to brave the cold temperatures and go out and share the love of Jesus Christ.

All the while, word of this was spreading throughout the state, and it led to the Time to Revive team being invited to seven different cities in Indiana over the course of the next seven months. We continued to witness the local body of believers in these various communities encouraged and equipped to continue to take out their faith and share with others. The gospel wasn't intended to stay only in the church building. Jesus commissioned each one of us to go and make disciples in our own Jerusalem, Judea, and Samaria and to the ends of the earth.

Back in Goshen, the local body continued to go out regularly after those initial 52 days while keeping track of the days since that first amazing week. A couple of years later in 2017, the local believers invited our team to celebrate their 1,000th day of outreach in their community. It was during that time when a local man shared with us a dream he had, which led us to start a two-year Bible study in the community. Similar to the Apostle Paul as he taught 12 disciples in Ephesus to study the Word of God on a daily basis, Time to Revive's desire was to also provide in-depth teaching that would focus on where the Messiah is found in every book of the Bible from Genesis to Revelation. We knew this would deepen their commitment to sharing the gospel as well as deepen their relationship with the Lord and with those whom they were discipling.

> But when some became hardened and would not believe, slandering the Way in front of the crowd, he withdrew from them and met separately with the disciples, conducting discussions every day in the lecture hall of Tyrannus. —Acts 19:9

This local Bible study started with 12 men who signed up and committed to study the Word of God in a barn on a county road in Goshen, Indiana. And on January 1, 2018, we launched reviveSCHOOL with 54 men in this initial group. They studied the Scriptures daily, using the online resources, then gathered in the barn to discuss them in person. Each student studied the Bible daily using these resources:

- a Scripture reading plan to stay on track,
- a 29-minute teaching video (by Kyle Lance Martin, Indiana pastors, and TTR teachers),
- a devotion (written by Laura Kim Martin),
- reading guide questions to help facilitate discussion and critical thinking,
- lesson plans to summarize the daily teaching, and
- a painting of each book of the Bible by Mindi Oaten.

Upon the completion of the two-year study in the Word, Time to Revive celebrated over 200 students who had joined reviveSCHOOL with a graduation ceremony in January 2020. Plans were made for these individuals to take the Word and launch reviveSCHOOL groups not only in the United States but also throughout various nations. However, with worldwide travel restrictions due to the COVID-19 pandemic, this travel didn't happen. Thankfully, God had another plan, His plan was "above and beyond" all that Time to Revive could ask or think of (Ephesians 3:20–21).

With all the reviveSCHOOL materials already available online, the Holy Spirit spread the word to pastors and leaders of nations all throughout the world. Believers were hungry for biblically sound teaching and resources to grow closer to the Lord. As exemplified in Acts 19 with Paul and the disciples, and all the people of Asia, the Word of God through reviveSCHOOL truly spread—from a barn in Indiana to the nations.

> And this went on for two years, so that all the inhabitants of Asia, both Jews and Greeks, heard the message about the Lord. —Acts 19:10

By God's grace, reviveSCHOOL has become an outlet for individuals to gain fresh insight into the Messiah all throughout the Scriptures, as well as to develop an understanding of the role of Israel from a biblical perspective.

I am humbled and honored that you would select reviveSCHOOL for your learning. When we started with 12 guys in a Bible study, we had no idea that reviveSCHOOL would be as far reaching as it has become. Our team would delight in knowing that you are studying the Word of God and using the resources with reviveSCHOOL. We pray that through these resources you will grow closer to the Lord and that you are inspired to walk out the plans that God has for your life by exposing others to the love of Christ.

To God be the glory!
Dr. Kyle Lance Martin

For further information about how to sign up for this two-year study in the Word of God or if you would like to launch a reviveSCHOOL group in your community, state/province, or country, please go online to www.reviveSCHOOL.org.

How to Use this Bible Study Series

The *Complete Portrait of the Messiah* Bible study series contains multiple components for each lesson. These components work together to provide an in-depth study of how Jesus is revealed throughout the whole of Scripture. Below is a description of each component and how you can use each one to maximize your study experience.

Teaching Notes and Video Lessons
The teaching notes summarize the main points of each video lesson and include a QR code to access the video teaching. If you have access to the internet via your phone, you can scan the QR code to watch the video lesson.*

The Daily Word Devotional
Dig deeper into personal application for each lesson through *The Daily Word* devotional. This day-by-day devotional encourages you with thoughts for application and further Scripture readings.

Reading Guide Questions
These questions will guide you into a more detailed exploration of each lesson's content. Examine the concepts of the daily Scripture readings in more detail.

The Bible Art Collection
This Bible study series is augmented by a one-of-a-kind, especially inspired series of original artwork created by artist Mindi Oaten. These 66 acrylic paintings creatively depict the revelation of Christ in each book of the Bible. Viewing each of these original art pieces will inspire your understanding and further enrich your understanding of Jesus throughout all of the Scriptures. These can be found at https://www.mindioaten.com/pages/mindi-oaten-art-bible-art-collection or https://www.reviveschool.org/

About the Cover

Hosea
"Our Faithful Husband"

Artist Notes: Mindi Oaten

Hosea's life served as a parable of God's faithfulness to the unfaithful nation of Israel. His love for us is greater than our "adulterous" ways. Jesus drew us to Himself by showing His love for us on the cross. His sacrifice made a way to connect us back to the Father in fellowship, the way God always intended. He is our bridegroom, our faithful husband, who will never leave us no matter how much we stray. Jesus is *Unconditional Love.*

Background / Scene of Wedding/ Round Table:

To go with the central metaphor of marriage in the book, I decided to paint a wedding table, a round one often used at weddings. Because we are talking about Israel, I went with a more Jewish theme. I like the symbol of a circle as well, it represents how God can restore and bring things "full circle."

Canopy / Chuppah:

In Jewish weddings, a chuppah is central in the ceremony. Often it is four posts with a canopy draped over and positioned at the place where the bride and groom will say their vows. A prayer cloth is used most often. This is symbolic of the home that the new couple will build together.

> The chuppah represents a Jewish home symbolized by the cloth canopy and the four poles. Just as a chuppah is open on all four sides, so was the tent of Abraham open for hospitality. Thus, the chuppah represents hospitality to one's guests. This "home" initially lacks furniture as a reminder that the basis of a Jewish home is the people within it, not the possessions. In a spiritual sense, the covering of the chuppah represents the presence of God over the covenant of marriage. (Wikipedia)

Thorns and Thistles:

"Therefore, this is what I will do:
I will block her way with thorns;
I will enclose her with a wall,
so that she cannot find her paths." (Hosea 2:6)

"The high places of Aven, the sin of Israel,
will be destroyed;
thorns and thistles will grow over their altars.
They will say to the mountains, 'Cover us!'
and to the hills, 'Fall on us!'" (Hosea 10:8)

Thorns and thistles often symbolize desolation and wilderness in the Bible. Thorns and thistles in the original curse of sin (Genesis 3:18) are a symbolic reminder of the things that choke out the fruit in our lives, the things that wound instead of nourish. In Hosea, we see thorns and thistles being used to describe blockage, hardship, and judgment. I painted thorns on the left side of the painting to represent this part of the book.

Wine Pitcher and Two Wine Glasses:

In Jewish tradition, the first wine cup is used at the betrothal blessing, by the rabbi. The second cup is when the couple drinks from one cup after they recite the blessings at the wedding. I chose to have the second cup tipped over and spilled out to symbolize Hosea's prostitute wife, the unfaithful wife, whom the Lord told him to marry. But at the same time, it symbolizes the union of the two, which God can and will restore. He will restore his unfaithful bride.

Hosea mentions wine in several places.

Red Ribbon:

"I led them with human cords,
with ropes of love.
To them I was like one
who eases the yoke from their jaws;
I bent down to give them food." (Hosea 11:4)

The red ribbon represents the ties of love. Whenever I've painted a red ribbon, I also use it to symbolize Jesus' blood as a ribbon of love.

Two Gold Rings:

These rings represent the covenant between God and His people.

Figs, Grapes, Olives (Oil), and Wheat:

"She does not recognize
that it is I who gave her the grain,
the new wine, and the oil.
I lavished silver and gold on her,
which they used for Baal." (Hosea 2:8)

"On that day I will respond—
    this is the LORD's declaration.
I will respond to the sky,
and it will respond to the earth.
The earth will respond to the grain,
the new wine, and the oil,
and they will respond to Jezreel." (Hosea 2:21–22)

Grain, new wine, and oil are mentioned in Hosea. In God's mercy to Israel, the land will one day flourish and be restored. Israel's adultery will be rebuked.

Grape Vines:

"Israel is a lush vine;
it yields fruit for itself.
The more his fruit increased,
the more he increased the altars.
The better his land produced,
the better they made the sacred pillars." (Hosea 10:1)

"The people will return and live beneath his shade.
They will grow grain
and blossom like the vine.
His renown will be like the wine of Lebanon." (Hosea 14:7)

Vines are mentioned in Hosea as a symbol of abundance. They were spoken of both positively and negatively. Because of their prosperity, Israel turned to idols through their wealth and abundance. In this verse, God restored Israel's blessings after they repented.

Flowers—Violets and Lily's: faithfulness

"I will be like the dew to Israel;
he will blossom like the lily
and take root like the cedars of Lebanon." (Hosea 14:5)

Violets are a symbol of modesty, spiritual wisdom, faithfulness, and humility. Lilies symbolize modesty and purity.

*In reviveSCHOOL, the theme name for Jesus in Hosea is *Unconditional Love*.

Lesson 1: Hosea 1—4

Unconditional Love: Hosea's Marriage and Children

Teaching Notes

Intro

Today, we're starting a new segment on the 12 books known as the Minor Prophets. The main difference between the major and minor prophets is the length of their prophecies. The Major Prophets include Isaiah, Jeremiah, Ezekiel, and Daniel, as well as the book of Lamentations, since it was written by Jeremiah. Today, we'll focus on the book of Hosea. Hosea's name means "salvation." His name foreshadows both Joshua and Jesus, whose names also imply "salvation." As we explore these minor prophets, we'll feel like we're back in captivity under the Assyrians and Babylonians.

Hosea was written in the language of the Northern Kingdom, ten of the tribes of Israel. The Southern Kingdom included the tribes of Judah and Benjamin, and the city of Jerusalem. We know the author is Hosea, but we don't know much about him or his father, Beeri (Hosea 1:1). John MacArthur said, "Hosea was probably a native of the Northern Kingdom of Israel, since he shows familiarity with the history, circumstances, and topography of the north . . . Although he addressed both Israel (the Northern Kingdom) and Judah, (the Southern Kingdom), he identified the king of Israel as 'our king' (7:5)."[1] Hosea's ministry was long—from 760 BC to 715 BC. During this time, the kings of the Southern Kingdom included Uzziah, Jotham, Ahaz, and Hezekiah. At the same time, he ministered during the reigns of the last six kings of Israel from Zechariah to Hoshea.[2]

Hosea followed Amos' preaching in the Northern Kingdom. He ministered during the same time frame as Isaiah and Micah. To put this in perspective, Isaiah wrote about the Babylonian captivity, but never experienced it. While 586 BC is an important date because it's when the Southern Kingdom fell into Babylonian captivity, the date we will see more often in the minor prophets is 722 BC, when

---

[1] John MacArthur, *The MacArthur Bible Commentary* (Nashville: Thomas Nelson, 2005), 970.

[2] MacArthur, 970.

the Northern Kingdom fell to the Assyrians. Another important thing to remember about the northern and southern kingdoms is they were not spiritually great. The only king who might have offered any hope was Hezekiah. Hosea spoke truth in a hard environment.

According to MacArthur, Hosea has been called the "St. John" of the Old Testament because John was known as the apostle of love.[3] Hosea uses the phrase "*Unconditional Love*" in his writings. Hosea 11:1 describes how much God loves His people. Hosea shows God's love for His covenant people in spite of their idolatry. Really, Hosea was a foreshadow of what Christ did for us. Throughout the book, there's a theme of "sin, judgment, and forgiving love."[4] This theme points us to Romans 5:8, "But God proves His own love for us in that while we were still sinners, Christ died for us!" Regardless of our spiritual adultery, Christ died for us and loves us unconditionally regardless of what we have done.

Teaching

Hosea 1:1–2: God told Hosea to marry a promiscuous wife. Tom Constable described several possible interpretations for this verse: Maybe, "God gave Hosea a vision, or that He told him an allegory, in which his wife was or would become a harlot."[5] Maybe she was a spiritual harlot because she worshipped a false God. Maybe she was sexually promiscuous before Hosea married her. Or maybe she became unfaithful after they got married.[6] Regardless of the specifics of her unfaithfulness, God wanted Hosea to stay faithful to his spouse.

Hosea 1:3–5: As we read this, we have to picture Hosea in the place of God, and Gomer in the place of the Israelites. Hosea's first son was named Jezreel. Remember, names are super-important in Scripture. Jezreel means "God will scatter." Prophetically, this makes us think of the fact that when the Assyrians conquered Israel, they were scattered among the nations. This was a prophetic word about the Assyrian conquest "on that day" in 722 BC.

Hosea 1:6–7: Gomer then bore a daughter who was named Lo-ruhamah, which means "no compassion." God warned that He would have no compassion on Israel. The girl's name also meant "unpitied," so He would have no pity for Israel. In contrast, God said He would have compassion on the house of Judah (v. 7). In 701 BC, God showed this compassion to Judah when 185,000 Assyrians were

---

[3] MacArthur, 971.

[4] MacArthur, 971.

[5] Thomas L. Constable, *Expository Notes of Dr. Thomas Constable:* Hosea, 20, https://planobiblechapel. org/tcon/notes/pdf/hosea.pdf.

[6] Constable, 21.

killed (2 Kings 19). Yes, God still loved His people, but He wanted them to know He was not pleased with them.

Hosea 1:8–10: When the daughter was weaned (no longer dependent on her mother's milk), Gomer conceived and bore another son. He was named, Lo-ammi, which means "Not My People." Although it sounds like God is break-ing covenant with His people, He is actually just allowing them to suffer the consequences for their unfaithfulness to Him. Because of God's *Unconditional Love* for Israel, even as He said, "You are not My people," He also said, "they will be called: Sons of the living God" (v. 10). Even in their unfaithfulness, God raised up a remnant who would be faithful to Him. When is this going to hap-pen? This sure sounds like the millennial blessing. Hosea was not talking about the first coming, because clearly Israel did not embrace Christ. Hosea had to be talking about the second coming that comes after the seven years of tribulation. This is when Israel will begin to understand that they are the sons of the living God. Romans 8:14 says, "All those led by God's Spirit are God's sons." At some point, the Jewish people will embrace this. When they believe in Yeshua, they will receive the Spirit of God and will identify themselves as sons and daughters of God.

Hosea 1:11: This is how we know Hosea was talking about the millennial bless-ing. At some point, all of the 12 tribes of Israel and Judah will gather together and appoint for themselves a single ruler. They are referencing the coming Messiah—not the first time Jesus came—but the second coming of Christ.

   Love this picture: God is going to scatter them, but now they are all coming together again. They will have a king—a single ruler—who will show *Uncondi-tional Love* for all of them.

Hosea 2:1—4:19: J. Vernon McGee gives an overview of these chapters. Gomer proves faithless. Israel proves faithless. And yet God proves faithful.[7] In Hosea 3, when Gomer did bad things, God told Hosea to show love to his wife regardless. According to Levitical law, Gomer should have been stoned. But this *Uncondi-tional Love* overcame all of these sins. In Hosea 4, Gomer turning away from Hosea is a picture of Israel turning away from God. Hosea, embracing his wife regardless, is a picture of God embracing Israel regardless. In Hosea 4, Israel con-tinues to play the harlot. They are guilty of lawlessness and immorality. They are ignorant of God's Word and they don't care.[8] There is no truth, no faithful love, and no knowledge of God in the land (Hosea 4:1). Israel is clearly backslidden

---

[7] J. Vernon McGee, *Hosea and Joel*, Thru the Bible Commentary Series (Nashville: Thomas Nelson, 1975, 1991), n.p.

[8] McGee, n.p.

and obstinate as a stubborn cow (Hosea 4:16). Despite God loving Israel, Israel doesn't care.

Closing

Despite Hosea loving Gomer she didn't care, just as God loves Israel, Israel at that time didn't seem to care. Hosea is a picture of unification, despite circumstances, through *Unconditional Love*. This is the backdrop for the book of Hosea.

The Daily Word

Hosea not only proclaimed prophetic messages for Israel but also lived them out in obedience to the Lord's instructions. Upon the Lord's command, Hosea married a promiscuous woman named Gomer. Although Gomer broke her marital promise to Hosea, he followed the Lord's command to love his adulteress wife in the same way God loved the Israelites who repeatedly turned to other gods.

Just as Hosea loved his wife again and again despite her unfaithfulness, the Lord demonstrated His love by sending His Son Jesus to die for you while you were still a sinner. When you believe in Jesus, you receive God's grace, unconditional love, and eternal life as a free gift. You didn't do anything to deserve Christ's love. He loves you as you are. *The love the Lord has for you never ends.* Even if you walk away from God, He will go again to you and show you love. God's love will never separate from you. In the same way, you are called to love others, even when they hurt you or walk away. You are called *to go again and show love*, just like Hosea loved Gomer. Today, go again and show Christ's love to those around you.

Then the LORD said to me, "Go again; show love to a woman who is loved by another man and is an adulteress, just as the LORD loves the Israelites though they turn to other gods and love raisin cakes." —Hosea 3:1

Further Scripture: Romans 5:8; 8:38–39; 1 John 4:19

Questions

1. How do you think you would handle a request from the Lord to marry a prostitute (as the Lord told Hosea in Hosea 1:2)?
2. How does Hosea 2 exemplify God's love for His children?
3. In Hosea 3:2, Hosea bought Gomer back for 15 pieces of silver, some barley, and wine. How did that compare to the price of a slave who had been injured in Exodus 21:32? Why do you think the price was so different?
4. What did the Holy Spirit highlight to you in Hosea 1—4 through the reading or the teaching?

Lesson 2: Hosea 5—8

Unconditional Love: False Repentance

Teaching Notes

Intro

Hosea is a minor prophet. The only difference between major prophets, (Isaiah, Jeremiah, Ezekiel, Daniel), and minor prophets is the length of the book. God asked Hosea to live out his prophetic ministry. God commanded Hosea to marry Gomer. Jezreel, meaning "God scatters" was their son. They later had a daughter whose named meant "No compassion," and a son named "Not my people." Even though God's people would be scattered, even though He wouldn't show them compassion, and even though they would be treated as if they were not His people, God constantly showed His people *Unconditional Love*. This was modeled in the life of Hosea.

Gomer was a promiscuous wife. We're not sure if she was promiscuous before they were married or if her behavior started after they were married. Either way, Gomer was unfaithful to Hosea. In the process of being unfaithful, she didn't value Hosea. Gomer became a picture of Israel who was unfaithful to the Lord and who didn't value Him. God led Hosea to unconditionally love his wife as a picture of how God loves His people.

Teaching

Hosea 5: As J. Vernon McGee noted, chapter 5 begins with a denunciation of Israel's leadership, both the priests and the king, by God.[1] Everyone in Israel would stumble because of their wickedness (v. 5). As tragedy began to strike the nation, the people would go looking for God, but God did not respond (v. 6). Even *Unconditional Love* can be tough love. Once Ephraim realized "his sickness," he turned to Assyria for help and not to the Lord (v. 13). This was the unfaithfulness represented by Gomer. Unfortunately for Israel, the king of Assyria "cannot cure you or heal your wound" (v. 13). God compared the judgment that would fall on Israel to a lion tearing them apart and carrying them away (v. 14). Afterwards,

---

[1] J. Vernon McGee, "Notes on Hosea," https://www.blueletterbible.org/Comm/mcgee_j_vernon/notes-outlines/hosea/hosea-outline.cfm.

God's presence would depart until Israel recognizes "their guilt and seek My face" (v. 15). Sometimes we have to hit absolute rock bottom before we are ready to repent and seek the Lord.

Hosea 6:1–3: The people of Israel spoke in the first three verses. They recognized that the damage that has been done to them has been at the Lord's hand: "He has torn us; He has wounded us" (v. 1). While they were technically correct, Wiersbe noted that the language used described "a nation's false repentance."[2] The people have not taken responsibility for their own sin. Their attitude seems to be, "Since God did this to us, He's going to have to fix it." While the people talked about knowing God and pursuing Him, there was a complete absence of repentance.

Hosea 6:4–6: God responded by comparing the Israelites' faithfulness to him to "the morning mist" and "dew that vanishes" (v. 4). God was more concerned with the condition of the Israelites' hearts and their relationship with Him than He was with the practice of their religion (v. 6). The Israelites could play the part, but God wanted more than just their religious observance. Samuel had expressed the same sentiment: "Then Samuel said, 'Does the Lord take pleasure in burnt offerings and sacrifices as much as in obeying the Lord? Look: to obey is better than sacrifice, to pay attention is better than the fat of rams. For rebellion is like the sin of divination, and defiance is like wickedness and idolatry. Because you have rejected the word of the Lord, He has rejected you as king'" (1 Samuel 15:22–23). David expressed the repentant attitude that the Lord sought: "You do not want a sacrifice, or I would give it; You are not pleased with a burnt offering. The sacrifice pleasing to God is a broken spirit. God, You will not despise a broken and humbled heart" (Psalm 51:15–16).

Hosea 6:7: God accused Israel of violating the covenant they made with Him. The covenant to which the Lord referred was the Mosaic covenant made between God and Israel at Mt. Sinai: "Now if you will listen to Me and carefully keep My covenant, you will be My own possession out of all the peoples, although all the earth is Mine, and you will be My kingdom of priests and My holy nation.' These are the words that you are to say to the Israelites" (Exodus 19:5–6). Israel's betrayal of their covenant with God was reminiscent of Adam's betrayal of God all the way back in the Garden (v. 7).

Hosea 6:8–11: Gilead and Shechem, referenced in verses 8–9 for the sins they committed, were meant to be cities of refuge. Israel's sin was so great that even the cities of refuge had become places that harbored sin. *Nelson's Commentary*

---

[2] Warren W. Wiersbe, *The Bible Exposition Commentary: Old Testament* (Colorado Springs: David C. Cook, 2002), 322.

points out that these were cities that were meant to provide calm environments in which people could find refuge, but they have become contaminated with sin.[3] If it could get worse, God had personally witnessed His people's infidelity (v. 10). While the Lord singled out Israel (the Northern Kingdom) for their infidelity, MacArthur noted, "the prophet reminds them that they have a day of reckoning also awaiting them."[4]

God desired that Israel have a broken and contrite heart over their sin. But Israel was content to make a show of repentance and ask God to help them, even though they had no conviction of their own sin. Isaiah described the kind of heart that God requires: "For the High and Exalted One who lives forever, whose name is Holy says this: 'I live in a high and holy place, and with the oppressed and lowly of spirit, to revive the spirit of the lowly and revive the heart of the oppressed'" (Isaiah 57:15). Hosea portrayed the Israelites as lacking this kind of lowly and contrite heart. They were more concerned with how they would get out of the terrible situation in which they found themselves and they were counting on God to bail them out without repentance.

Hosea 7: In spite of everything, God promised that He would heal His people. But they would "be exposed" when healing came (v. 1). God had seen all of Israel's sins. As a result, they had "become like a silly, senseless dove" that bounced back and forth between Egypt and Assyria looking for relief (v. 11).

Hosea 8: God continued to depict Israel's unfaithfulness to Him. On top of everything else, they added idolatry to their offenses. God's frustration reached a high point: "How long will they be incapable of innocence (v. 5)"?

Closing

Isn't this how we function in we live a lifestyle of sin, looking for the next fix? It doesn't work. Hosea 6, 7, and 8, is about Israel faking it so they could keep having their fixes through sin! In spite of everything, God still loved His people. In obedience to his call, Hosea still loved Gomer.

The Daily Word

Just as God loved Israel, Hosea loved Gomer, despite her lack of loyalty in their marriage. As much as the Lord desired for Israel to repent, He called their bluff when they said: *Let us strive to know God. Let us return to the Lord, He will heal us.*

---

[3] Earl D. Radmacher, Ronald B. Allen, and H. Wayne House, eds., *Nelson's New Illustrated Bible Commentary* (Nashville: Thomas Nelson, 1999), 1032.

[4] John MacArthur, *The MacArthur Bible Commentary* (Nashville: Thomas Nelson, 2005), 977.

The Lord desired surrendered hearts, not external religion in which the people strove to act like they followed God. Despite their ungodly actions, the Lord remained patient, and His love for Israel continued.

In many ways, this same lip-service religion is offered to the Lord today. *The Lord wants your heart.* He desires *your loyalty* to Him. He wants you to draw near to Him. He doesn't want empty religious activity. He wants you to *love Him wholeheartedly.* Don't try fake repentance without a broken heart. Honestly turn to the Lord with full humility and authentically ask for forgiveness, desiring His love. Acknowledge He is the *only* one who can fill your cup, He is the *only* one to satisfy your longing, and He is the only one to heal you. But you must be real with Him. Come before Him today. Cease striving in your own strength. Be real. Be honest. Lay it all down before Him at the cross. Receive His love, and then walk in obedience.

For I desire loyalty and not sacrifice,
the knowledge of God rather than burnt offerings. —Hosea 6:6

Further Scripture: 1 Samuel 15:22; Psalm 51:16–17; Isaiah 57:15

Questions

1. Where else in Scripture is the latter and the former rain mentioned as in Hosea 6:3 (Joel 2:23; Acts 2:17–21)? Are there any differences between the two references?

2. Jesus said that love/mercy is more important than burnt offerings (Matthew 9:13; 12:7). Are those passages teaching the same thing as in Hosea 6:6? Why?

3. The people of Israel were compared to a half-baked cake (Hosea 7:8). What are the issues with a half-baked cake? Why were they compared to cake?

4. What did the Holy Spirit highlight to you in Hosea 5—8 through the reading or the teaching?

Lesson 3: Hosea 9—11

Unconditional Love: The Lord's Love for Israel

Teaching Notes

Intro

Hosea was one of the minor prophets. He was a prophet to the northern and southern kingdoms of Israel. God had Hosea go through a broad array of experiences as part of his prophecy. First, Hosea was told by God to marry Gomer. They had three children. The names of the children were indicative that God was scattering the Israelites and that He would not care for them in their present state. Gomer becomes promiscuous or was possibly a prostitute. And Hosea had to watch all this unfold.

Teaching

Hosea 11: God told Hosea that he had to unconditionally love his wife, who did not care him. Basically, his wife said to Hosea that he was not good enough for her. The image of Hosea and giving *Unconditional Love* to Gomer represents the image of God doing the same for Israel. God proved that He had *Unconditional Love* for Israel.

Israel was thick-headed. Hosea stated that Israel was like a stubborn cow. God said to Hosea that He would scatter his children and not care for them. They would either be killed or at least held in captivity.

On Hosea 11:9, J. Vernon McGee wrote that the verse referred to Israel as backsliding heifers:

> At this time, Israel was beginning to look to prosperity as the indication that everything was all right in the nation. In other words, they were trying to increase the value of their money, and they were attempting to increase the productivity of the land. But God said they were nothing but a backsliding heifer. He had blessed them with prosperity, and that had blinded them to the reality of their spiritual condition.[1]

---

[1] J. Vernon McGee, *Proverbs Through Malachi*, vol. 3 Thru the Bible (Nashville Thomas Nelson, 1983), 644.

They looked more to the land and its prosperity than to God.

Previously Israel had looked to false prophets and false religions. Now they had turned to prosperity and material possessions. Hosea compared Israel to a prostitute. Israel felt its security was in the land, but was about to lose the land. If Israel wanted to keep their lifestyle, it would lead to the nation's death and destruction. Parents would be handing their children over for death. Sinful lifestyles led to shorter life spans. MacArthur explains, "Agricultural prosperity had resulted in spiritual corruption (cf. Ezekiel 16:10–19)."[2] Israel had turned away from the Lord, its first love. God would ultimately judge the nation.

Hosea 11:1–4: Here is the picture of God loving His people so much that He took them out of Egypt. The people He brought out of Egypt would then be part of the lineage of Jesus. That explained why Hosea stated that the word from God was that, out of these people, He would call His son. What is seen through these passages is that God loved His people and God loved His Son. Both were pulled out of Egypt.

But the more that the people of Israel heard the truth, the more they sacrificed offerings to Baal and worshipped other idols. Hosea 12:10 explains that God spoke to the people through the prophets. But it appeared that the more Hosea spoke to the people, the more they left and turned away from God.

In verse 1, a progression started with the image of a child and a father. As God was with the people, He tried to teach them. The people had forgotten that God had given life to them. Israel was going after its own heart and Gomer was going after her own heart.

The image in verse 4 was that God led the people with ropes of love. *Nelson's Commentary* explains, "The image of v. 3 changes as God is compared to a farmer and Israel to a beast of burden. The Lord placed restraints—cords and bands—on Israel, but His regulations, rather than being overly strict or harsh, reflected His concern for the people's wellbeing."[3] God was showing them the path and the process.

Hosea 11:5–7: In verses 5–7, the Scripture addressed the punishment that was to come. The nation of Israel would not return to the land of Israel. There was not a humble spirit in the people. They refused to repent.

Verse 7 was the second reference of backsliding. There were three major references to backsliding in Hosea: 4:16, 11:7, and 14:4. The term "backslider" was often used by prophets. MacArthur explains that the term "is used here in such

---

[2] John MacArthur, *The MacArthur Bible Commentary* (Nashville: Thomas Nelson, 2005), 978.

[3] Earl D. Radmacher, Ronald B. Allen, and H. Wayne House, eds., *Nelson's New Illustrated Bible Commentary* (Nashville: Thomas Nelson, 1999), 978.

a way as to clarify who is a backslider. He belongs in the category of the fool, the wicked, and the disobedient and he is contrasted with the godly wise. It is a word that the prophets used of apostate unbelievers."[4] Jeremiah 3:6 gives reference to the prostitute and the unfaithful, in comparison to Israel.

Hosea 11:8–9: Verse 8 contains the theme verse for all of Hosea. God's compassion was stirred and His heart was touched. There was still sympathy for the people. Romans 5:8 referenced the same *Unconditional Love* as expressed in verse 8. God would not come to His people in rage.

Hosea 11:10–12: In verse 10, the image of God is a lion. It is a peaceful picture. Constable states, "In the future, the Israelites would follow the LORD (cf. vv. 2, 5). He would again announce His intentions like a roaring lion (Hosea 5:14; 13:7; Amos 1:2; 3:8). However, this time it would not be as a lion about to devour its prey, but as a lion leading its cubs to safety. The Israelites would follow Him, 'trembling from the west' (Hosea 3:5; Exodus 19:16)."[5]

The reference of the people coming from the west was of the people coming from all parts of the land and coming back to God. Coming from the east would have been a return from captivity. This was the gathering of people back into God's presence.

Closing

Hosea 11:8 is like a window into the heart of God, *Unconditional Love.* God's love would not let them go. This was a picture of the returning of God's children using the image of Hosea's children returning to him to explain it. The lion roaring was an image of God calling all people to come back to Him. Ultimately the people would return back to the land and back to God (Isaiah 11:11–12). It was a picture of hope. God's love would not let the people go.

The Daily Word

The Lord's compassion stirred despite Israel's rebellious spirit. God cared for His children. He yearned for them to come back to Him. His heart broke for them; therefore, He couldn't just give them up. He loved unconditionally, and nothing would separate that love. The Lord demonstrated mercy and grace to His children.

Hosea described God leading His children with "ropes of love" out of captivity in Egypt. Imagine a dad leading his son through a busy airport. For his son

---

[4] MacArthur, 712.

[5] Thomas L. Constable, *Expository Notes of Dr. Thomas Constable: Hosea*, 90, https://planobiblechapel. org/tcon/notes/pdf/hosea.pdf.

not to walk away and get lost, the son wears a backpack with a rope on it for the father to grasp. This is a picture of God's heart for you, His child. He loves you so much. He desires to lead you with ropes of love out of bondage by sending you Jesus, His only Son. God loves you unconditionally and will not let you go. No matter how long the ropes of love may go—*the Lord's love will never, ever let you go*. The Lord's compassion remains for you. When you think no one else cares, God cares, and He promises to be with you. His love is wide and high and deep. Today, will you receive His great love and allow the Lord to lead you?

How can I give you up, Ephraim?
How can I surrender you, Israel?
How can I make you like Admah?
How can I treat you like Zeboiim?
I have had a change of heart;
My compassion is stirred! —Hosea 11:8

Further Scripture: Hosea 11:1, 4; Romans 5:8; Ephesians 3:17–19

Questions

1. In Hosea 9:1, Hosea accused Israel of harlotry or whoredom. How does James 4:4 describe this kind of spiritual "adultery"? Does the Lord hold Israel to a different standard concerning idol worship than the other nations?

2. Read Hosea 9:16a and Mark 11:13–14, 20. How are these two passages similar? Do you think the passage in Mark could be symbolic as well as literal?

3. In Hosea 10:5, Hosea mentioned Beth-aven. The meaning of this name is believed to be "House of wickedness." Why did the Lord refer to the city of Bethel (House of God) as Beth-aven? What was significant about Bethel in the Old Testament? (Genesis 28:11–19; Judges 20:18, 26–28; Hosea 12:4)

4. In Luke 23:30, Jesus quoted Hosea 10:8. What was the situation at the time He quoted Hosea, and why do you think He quoted it?

5. When you read Hosea 10:12–13, do you think of Galatians 6:7–8? Do you see a pattern of Scripture using planting and reaping analogies? (Proverb 11:18; Hosea 10:13; Luke 6:38; 1 Corinthians 3:6–9; 2 Corinthians 9:6; Galatians 6:7–9)

6. In Matthew 2:15, the writer quoted Hosea 11:1. Who was Matthew referencing? Who else in Israel's past was called out of Egypt? How do you think Matthew recognized this as a messianic prophecy?

7. What did the Holy Spirit highlight to you in Hosea 9—11 through the reading or the teaching?

Lesson 4: Hosea 12—14

Unconditional Love: Repentance and Restoration

Teaching Notes

Intro

In Hosea, the two primary characters of the book were Hosea and his wife Gomer. They had three children, but she was not faithful to Hosea. In all of this, God asked Hosea to show *Unconditional Love* to his unfaithful wife. The lives of Hosea and Gomer represent God and unfaithful Israel. The bottom line is that Gomer, who represented the Israelites, was not faithful to Hosea, who represented God. Gomer refused to be faithful in the marriage just as the Israelites were unfaithful to God.

Teaching

Hosea 12: In Hosea 12:1, Ephraim made a covenant with Egypt to trade goods. The Israelites' unfaithfulness was shown in their dependence on their own prosperity. They put their trust in everything they would produce for themselves, rather than the Lord. They doubted the Lord's care for them.

The people claimed there was no crime in them, and that they were only doing what was necessary to survive. But the judgment of God caught up with them because they chose to put their trust in their own prosperity rather than in the promises of God.

J. Vernon McGee states,

> There is a prophetic sidelight here that is very interesting. In Daniel's vision (Daniel 7), Babylon is pictured as a lion, Greece (under Alexander the Great), is pictured as a leopard, and the empire of Media-Persia is pictured as the bear. Now here in Hosea's prophecy God is saying that in the future He will come against them like a lion and a leopard, but in the immediate future He will come like a bear represented by Media-Persia, which at that early date was dominated by Assyria.[1]

---

[1] J. Vernon McGee, *Proverbs Through Malachi*, vol. 3 of Thru the Bible (Nashville Thomas Nelson, 1983), 655.

The people of Israel had no help available but God. And they had chosen not to trust in Him.

God referred to King Saul and the fact that judgment was coming. Paul quoted Hosea 13:14 in I Corinthians 15:55. The only way the people of Israel could understand that death no longer had a grip was because through God they could be set free. God's love was unconditional.

Hosea 13: Hosea 13:14–16 is a reference to guilt and severe punishment. These verses provide the introduction to chapter 14. Constable states, "As usual in the major sections of Hosea, promises of restoration follow announcements of judgment. This final section of restoration promises begins with an appeal for repentance and closes with the prospect of full and complete restoration."[2]

Hosea 14:1–8: In verse 1, Hosea stressed having humility and a contrite spirit. If the people had truly repented, they would be allowed to walk in freedom through God. Despite their disobedience and lack of trust, the people could come back to the Lord at any time with true praise and repentance.

MacArthur explains, "Israel was invited to return, bringing words of repentance accompanied with obedience, repaying God's gracious acceptance of them with genuine 'sacrifices of our lips' (Hebrews 13:15). God condemns lip-service worship (Isaiah 29:13; Matthew 15:8)."[3] Hosea 14 was referring to genuine repentance and not lip service. God was going to do something about the circumstances with Israel. He was going to continue to love His people and free them from apostasy. He would heal their condition.

Israel was realizing they needed the Lord. Therefore, God's anger was turning away. God would provide new life. The source of their new life was God. Wiersbe outlined verses 2–5 as, "He will receive us (vv. 2–3), He will restore us (v. 4), and He will revive us (vv. 5–8)."[4] The people finally realized they needed repentance.

Constable explains the significance of these verses: "Israel would become productive and attractive to the eye and nose, namely: totally appealing. 'Shoots' imply stability, 'beauty' suggests visibility, and 'fragrance' connotes desirability."[5] The people would return to God. MacArthur states, "Their scent ('remembrance')

---

[2] Thomas L. Constable, *Expository Notes of Dr. Thomas Constable: Joshua*, 2, http://planobiblechapel.org/tcon/notes/pdf/joshua.pdf.

[3] MacArthur, 981.

[4] Warren W. Wiersbe, *The Bible Exposition Commentary: Isaiah–Malachi* (Colorado Springs, David C. Cook, 1989), 329, 330.

[5] Constable, 107.

denotes worldwide fame and admiration."[6] Constable points out that "other nations would also flourish as they benefited from Israel's good influence."[7]

Hosea 14:9: Now the Israelites realized that they should have nothing more to do with idols. Verse 9 represents a picture of all of Hosea.

Closing

The message of the book of Hosea is about God's *Unconditional Love* and it prefaced the message of Christ. Christ wanted to set everyone free in spite of sin. Romans 3:23 states all have sinned. Romans 6:23 is about sin leading to death. Romans 5:8 offers hope in God's love. Christ in His death offers the people salvation. Ephesians 2:8–9 states that salvation is a gift of God. Sin, death, love, faith, and life are the five words that described the message of Hosea. The name Hosea means "salvation."

Takeaways from Hosea include that the ways of the Lord are right. Hosea presented two conditions: (1) obedience, or (2) disobedience. The wise obey and the foolish disobey. Ultimately, despite their disobedience, God showed compassion because of His *Unconditional Love.*

The Daily Word

Hosea continued to love Gomer despite how she rejected him and loved others. Even though Gomer broke her marriage vow to Hosea, he remained willing to receive her when she returned to him. He loved her unconditionally. The Lord God loves Israel unconditionally. Despite their covenant with God, Israel rejected Him and worshipped other gods. Even so, Israel can always return to Yahweh their God. The Lord will *receive their repentance and restore them to new life rooted in Him.*

Do you need this truth today? No matter how many times you have turned against God and sought other idols, the Lord's love remains. Do you hear His voice calling you back to Him? Do you have a tug in your heart to turn to Him in humility as your one source for love and satisfaction? Turn to the *one,* Jesus Christ, and His *Unconditional Love.* He will heal you. He will restore you. He will give you new life. Take root in Him, and He will bring you growth. You will blossom in new ways as you surrender completely to Him. Today, surrender and ask the Lord to be the king of your heart.

---

[6] MacArthur, 981.

[7] Constable, 107.

> Israel, return to Yahweh your God,
> for you have stumbled in your sin.
> Take words of repentance with you
> and return to the Lord.
> Say to Him: "Forgive all our sin
> and accept what is good,
> so that we may repay You
> with praise from our lips." —Hosea 14:1–2

Further Scripture: Hosea 14:4–7a, 9; Ephesians 2:8–9

Questions

1. Where else in Scripture can you find the story of Jacob wrestling with God (Genesis 32:24–30)? What do you think that looked like? Was it God Himself? In Genesis 32:30, Jacob said he saw God face to face. What do you think he meant by this, since John 1:18 and 4:12 both say that no one has ever seen God at any time? (Deuteronomy 5:4; 34:10)

2. In Hosea 13:11, what king is Hosea referring to (1 Samuel 9:15–17)? Why do you suppose the people wanted an earthly leader to rule over them as opposed to God Himself? How is this similar to today's political/worldly view?

3. How is Hosea 13:14 a prediction of Jesus' saving grace? (1 Corinthians 15:55–56)

4. What was Hosea saying in Hosea 14:9? (Job 34:10–12; Romans 9:32–33)

5. What did the Holy Spirit highlight to you in Hosea 12—14 through the reading or the teaching?

Lesson 5: Joel 1—3

Avenger: Judgment of the Nations

Teaching Notes

Intro

This week, we've already looked at Hosea, one of the minor prophets. Hosea clearly had a word for the Israelites, both in the northern and the southern kingdoms. This is the first and only lesson on the minor prophet, Joel. The book of Joel is truly one of a kind. Joel's name means, "the Lord of God," and there were at least 12 men in the Old Testament, and one in the New Testament, with the name Joel. In Joel 1:1, the author was identified as "Joel the son of Pethuel."

MacArthur points out that, "Although Joel displayed a profound zeal for the temple sacrifices (Joel 1:9; 2:13–16), his familiarity with pastoral and agricultural life and his separation from the priests (Joel 1:13,14; 2:17), suggest he was not a Levite."[1] However, extrabiblical writings state that Joel was a member of the tribe of Reuben and from the town of Bethom or Bethharam, which was located to the northwest on the border of Reuben and Gad. Evidence within the book itself suggests that Joel was Judean and from Jerusalem. This is based on the fact that he did not write from the perspective of a stranger.[2]

The book's date is based on where it was placed in the canon of Scripture, as well as on historical evidence within the book and the book's language and grammar. MacArthur explains that, "Because of: (1) the lack of any explicit mention of later world powers (Assyria, Babylon, or Persia); (2) the fact that Joel's style is like that of Hosea and Amos, rather than of the post-exilic prophets; and (3) the verbal parallels with other early prophets (Joel 3:16/Amos 1:2; Joel 3:18/Amos 9:13), a late-ninth-century-BC date during the reign of Joash (c. 835–796 BC), seems most convincing."[3] Interestingly, J. Vernon McGee suggests that Joel would have known both Elijah and Elisha.[4]

---

[1] John MacArthur, *The MacArthur Bible Commentary* (Nashville: Thomas Nelson, 2005), 982.

[2] MacArthur, 982.

[3] MacArthur, 982.

[4] J. Vernon McGee, "Notes for Joel," https://www.blueletterbible.org/Comm/mcgee_j_vernon/notes-outlines/joel/joel-notes.cfm.

According to Joel 3:2–4, Tyre, Sidon, and Philistia had made military attacks into Israel. MacArthur explains that "an extended drought and massive invasion of locusts had stripped every green thing from the land and brought severe economic devastations (Joel 1:7–20), leaving the Southern Kingdom weak."[5] Joel used the locust invasion as an example of God's coming judgment on sin and "God's future judgments during the Day of the Lord [that] will far exceed them."[6] Of the eight Old Testament authors who used the phrase "the day of the Lord" a total of 19 times, Joel put the most emphasis on it. There are four other uses of it in the New Testament. Joel was the prominent prophet on the Day of the Lord, and his prophecy will tie into Matthew and Revelation. The Day of the Lord will come "possibly due to a calloused indifference" to the Lord.[7]

MacArthur explains that the Day of the Lord is not always used as foretelling as eschatological event. It can also be used to explain "a near historical fulfillment" (Ezekiel 13:5). The Day of the Lord is often used to explain "seismic disturbances, violent weather, clouds and thick darkness, cosmic upheaval, and as a 'great and very terrible' (Joel 2:11) day that would 'come as destruction from the Almighty' (Joel 1:15)," as well as point to the promise of hope and "a pouring out of the Spirit on all flesh."[8]

Our phrase for Joel is *Avenger*. In Joel, the nations will come together in the Valley of Jehoshaphat at the end of the seven years of tribulation on the Day of the Lord to fight against Israel and King Jesus. Jesus will serve as the *Avenger* (Joel 3:19- 21) and will exact satisfaction for doing wrong by punishing the person who did wrong. Jesus will come in the end times and avenge those who have done wrong against the nations.

Teaching

Joel 1:1–14: Joel prophesied of the plague of locusts. He described 4 types of locust who would continue destroy everything. In verse 5, the locusts even destroyed the vineyards. In verses 6–7, Joel compared the locusts to an invading army. The invading army will totally destroy everything (vv. 8–10). Joel outlined ten groups who would mourn and suffer because of the locusts: drunkards, farmers, fruit growers, priests, ministers of the altar, the ministers of God, the residents/elders of the land in worship, and the entire assembly. They will all cry out to the Lord for help (vv. 9–14).

---

[5] MacArthur, 982.

[6] MacArthur, 982.

[7] MacArthur, 982.

[8] MacArthur, 983.

Joel 1:15—2:32: Joel said the Day of the Lord was near, and His judgment would come. Verses 16–20 describe the results of the plague. In Joel 2:1–10, Joel told them to sound the alarm because the Day of the Lord was near and then described what the Great Tribulation would be like. Darkness will cover the earth before Christ comes. In verses 12–17, Joel said there would be one last call for repentance. Verse 14 calls for a remnant. God called for the people to return to Him. Verses 18–19 give God's blessings, and then God will begin to drive back the invading armies (vv. 20–24). God will bring restoration to the land (vv. 26–27). Verses 28–32 was quoted by Peter (Acts 2:16–21), and promised the pouring out of God's Spirit on His people.

Joel 3:1–10: God will restore the fortunes of His people and then gather the nations in the Valley of Jehoshaphat. He will judge the nations who did not treat the Jewish nation right (vv. 1–6). The Jews had been sold into slavery, and forced into prostitution for money or pleasure. The temple treasures of gold and silver had been stolen and the people of Judah and Jerusalem had been sold to foreign masters and deported from their lands. God promised to bring retribution against these, bring His people back, and then do to these nations what they had done to the Jews (vv. 7–8). God told the Gentile nations to prepare for a holy war (v. 9). These nations were to beat the plows into swords and their pruning knives into spears. Even the weaklings would be needed as warriors (v. 10).

Joel 3:11–21: God told them to come quickly, for there He would judge them all (vv. 11–13). Joel said the Day of the Lord is near and multitudes would come to the valley for His decision because the Day of the Lord is near (v. 14). This refers to the Battle of Armageddon. The sun and moon will grow dark and even the stars will not shine (v. 15). The Lord will roar from Zion and heaven and earth will shake. And the Lord will be a refuge for His people, the Jews (v. 16).

Through this, everyone will know that God is the God of the Israelites, and that Jerusalem is His holy city (v. 17). Verse 18 is a picture of the temple flowing with water described in Ezekiel 47:1–5. Egypt and Edom will be desolated for their actions to the people of Judah (v. 19). And Judah and Jerusalem will be inhabited forever (v. 20). God will pardon their bloodguilt, for He dwells in Zion (v. 21) (Genesis 12:3; Matthew 25—sheep and goat nations.

Closing

The beauty of this picture is that God will always have our backs when we repent, we turn to Him, when we cry out to the Lord and pray. Jesus serves as the *Avenger* for those that choose to go against us.

The Daily Word

Joel instructed God's people to gather and blow the trumpet—for the day of the Lord is coming! Locusts invaded the land of Israel causing destruction, but the Lord came to restore. A great army rose up against Israel because they did not seek the Lord. But even so, the Lord restored His people. The Lord provided plenty to eat, and they were satisfied. If His people will praise the name of Yahweh, they will never again be put to shame. The great I Am is present in Israel, and He is their God. There is *no other* god. The Lord will display wonders among His people. And everyone who calls upon the name of the Lord will be saved.

Are you ready for the day of the Lord? God may bring destruction, but He will bring you restoration. He will satisfy you when you turn to Him. All the nations will gather and know there are no other gods besides the one true God, the Great Redeemer. His Spirit will move miraculously—through dreams, visions, prophecies, and wonders in the heavens and on earth. Just as Christ came to love all, you are called to love like Christ. From the place of His love flowing through you, His Spirit will move so the whole world will proclaim that Jesus Christ is Lord. Today, *stand firm and ready yourself* for the day of the Lord.

You will have plenty to eat and be satisfied.
You will praise the name of Yahweh your God,
who has dealt wondrously with you.
My people will never again be put to shame.
You will know that I am present in Israel
and that I am Yahweh your God,
and there is no other.
My people will never again be put to shame. —Joel 2:26–27

Further Scripture: Psalm 22:26; Isaiah 44:6; Joel 2:28–30a

Questions

1. How does Joel 1:1–4 and 7 compare to Amos 4:9–10? Were the two prophets speaking to the same audience at the same time? In general, do you think people learn from their past mistakes? What does this say about God's mercy toward us?

2. In Joel 1:13–14, what did the prophet Joel tell the people to do? Do you believe the Church would be in a better state today if we did more of this?

3. What does God promise to do if God's people repent and turn their hearts back to Him? (Joel 2:12–13)

4. Who in the New Testament, quoted the prophet Joel's words in Joel 2:28–32 (Acts 2:14–21)? Why did he quote them? What was happening?
5. What did the Holy Spirit highlight to you in Joel 1—3 through the reading or the teaching?

Lesson 6: Amos 1—3

Restorer: Reason for Punishing Israel

Teaching Notes

Intro

There are 12 minor prophets including Amos. He was in the northern province. His name meant *burden*. Amos was an everyday person from a small village ten miles south of Jerusalem named Tekoa.

Amos was the only prophet to announce his occupation before he was called to be a prophet. He was a sheep breeder and not of priestly or noble descent. God used everyday people to bring His Word. He stated he was not a prophet or the son of a prophet. So basically, he took care of trees and sheep. Acts 4:13 gave the account of the men that followed Jesus. The passage outlined the qualifications of Peter and John. They were uneducated and untrained regular people, but they had been in the presence of Jesus.

Amos' writing took place while Jeroboam II was king, between 793 and 753 BC. He wrote two years before a memorable earthquake. Zechariah mentioned the earthquake 200 years after it had happened as referenced in Zechariah 14:5.

MacArthur stated,

> Amos was a Judean prophet called to deliver a message primarily to the northern tribes of Israel (Amos 7:15). Politically, it was a time of prosperity for Israel under the long and secure reign of Jeroboam II who, following the example of his father Joash (2 Kings 13:25), significantly 'restored the territory of Israel' (2 Kings 14:25). It was also a time of peace with both Judah (cf. 5:5) and her more distant neighbors; the ever-present menace of Assyria was subdued, possibly because of Nineveh's repentance at the preaching of Jonah (Jonah 3:10). Spiritually, however, it was a time of rampant corruption and moral decay (Amos 4:1; 5:10–13; 2 Kings 14:24).[1]

---

[1] John MacArthur, *The MacArthur Bible Commentary* (Nashville: Thomas Nelson, 2005), 992.

Amos 4:1 was an example of the decay of their spirituality where wealthy women oppressed the poor and crushed the needy. Amos had two messages to bring. There was a lack of true justice and lack of true worship. According to MacArthur, "In the midst of their ritualistic performance of worship, they were not pursuing the Lord with their hearts (Amos 4:4–5; 5:4–6), nor following His standard of justice with their neighbors (Amos 5:10–13; 6:12)."[2] There were no standards.

As prophets were giving the Word from God, no one wanted to hear from them. In Amos 9, there was reference to what a *Restorer* would look like. In Amos 9:11–15 God said He would restore all that He had promised. It was a foreshadowing of what Christ would do in their lives. God showed what a *Restorer* looked like. The Lord declared that He would bring about the restoration.

Teaching

Amos 1:1–5: Chapter 1 started with a description of Amos, who he was, and what he would do. The first of several judgments that were to come was addressed in verses 3–5. Judgment would come against Syria and specifically to Damascus, the capital city, for cruelty. The crimes of Syria were numerous and along the lines of ungodliness in the worst form.

Amos 1:6–8: the Lord would not relent from punishing the nations. In Gaza, a city in Philistia, their crimes were in regards to their role in oppression and opposition to God's people. They were making slaves of the people.

Amos 1:9–10: The pattern of Scripture in the first verses of chapter 1 were repeated in verses 9–10. Judgment was coming against Tyre in the region of Phoenicia, along the Mediterranean.

Amos 1:11–12: By verses 11–12 God had told Hosea to tell the people that He would judge all these cities. McGee stated, "The judgment against Edom is because of their revengeful spirit. Back of revenge one ordinarily finds jealousy. The Edomites were jealous of their brothers."[3]

Amos 1:13–15: In verses 13–15 judgment came against the Ammonites for their cruelty and violent crimes. Rabbah was the capital city of Ammon

---

[2] MacArthur, 992.

[3] J. Vernon McGee, *The Prophets: Amos and Obadiah*, vol. 28 of Thru the Bible (Nashville: Thomas Nelson, 1995), n.p.

Amos 2:1–3: Chapter 2 continues the list of cities that would be judged by God. Moab was the next city mentioned that would face judgment because of their disrespect of the dead royalty. Verses 1–3 in chapter 2 fit better with chapter 1.

Amos 2:4–5: There was a shift in verses 4–5. Hosea now addressed the judgment that would come to Judah and Israel. The judgment was no longer about the surrounding nations. The kings and prophets had rejected the instruction of the Lord. Israel was no different from the other cities that were facing judgment. Their leaders led the people astray. There was no respect for the instruction and the Law of God.

Amos 2:6–16: These verses specifically addressed the judgment that was to come against Israel. The sins of Israel were no different from the sins of the other cities, every statement of judgment against every city mentioned, three crimes, maybe four, that had been committed against God and God's people.

Amos 3:1–2: Chapter 3 implies that God had an intimate and chosen relationship with the people of Israel. Yet, Israel was guilty of multiple sins against God including immorality, blasphemy, and various other sins. McGee said, "This is a great principle that God puts down here. He intends to judge in a harsher manner those who have received light than those who are in darkness."[4] Israel should know God's way. The Israelites disobeyed to the extent that judgment was now coming. They had abandoned God's standard.

Amos 3:3–8: Next, five questions are raised that should receive a negative answer, and two questions are raised that should get a positive answer. Constable said,

> Amos asked seven rhetorical questions in verses 3–6 to help the Israelites appreciate the inevitability of their judgment. In each one, the prophet pointed out that a certain cause inevitably produces a certain effect. The five questions in verses 3–5 expect a negative answer, and the two in verse 6 expect a positive one. Verses 7–8 draw the conclusion. The comparisons start out peacefully (two people walking together), but increase in intensity (to a city under attack). This creates an ominous rhetorical tone.[5]

God was going to reveal Himself to His people and He did that through the prophet Amos. He forewarned His people of His judgment.

---

[4] McGee, n.p.

[5] Thomas L. Constable, *Expository Notes of Dr. Thomas Constable: Amos*, 34, https://planobiblechapel.org /tcon/notes/pdf/amos.pdf.

The people were not capable of doing right. Pagan nations appeared to be more righteous than Israel. Judgment was going to come to Israel in the form of adversaries that would punish them.

Closing

Amos implied there would be a small remnant of Israel that would remain after the judgment. God seemed to be fed up with His people. God would destroy their false religions. And because of their misuse of wealth, Israel would face judgment. The message had not changed, God expected obedience. Eventually, God would still show up and restore the situation and His people.

The Daily Word

The Lord called Amos, a sheep breeder from Tekoa, and gave him a prophetic message to proclaim to Israel. The message described punishment for Israel and its neighbors. Over and over, Amos said God would not relent in punishing, judging, and destroying these nations because they had turned against the Lord. Amos repeatedly declared God would "send fire . . . and it will consume."

Even today the Lord is a consuming fire in your life. The Lord sees when you worship other gods or when you seek satisfaction from the world instead of seeking Him first. God loves you unconditionally, but *He is a jealous God*. He longs for you to worship and love Him above all else. He longs for you to revere and stand in awe of who He is. He may take you through a trial *so His fire can bring refinement to create you into who He's called you to be for His purpose in His kingdom*. When you walk through fiery trials, know the Lord your God is with you. Seek Him in the fire. He is there. Praise His name even through the heat. Allow Him to burn off anything in your life not of Him. Praise the name of the Lord as your restorer and redeemer. You will not be shaken.

I will not relent from punishing Judah
for three crimes, even four,
because they have rejected the instruction of the Lord
and have not kept His statutes.
The lies that their ancestors followed
have led them astray.
Therefore, I will send fire against Judah,
and it will consume the citadels of Jerusalem. —Amos 2:4–5

Further Scripture: Deuteronomy 4:23–24; Isaiah 33:14; Hebrews 12:28–29

Questions

1. In Amos 1 and the beginning of Amos 2, what were the six Gentile nations that Amos pronounced judgment on?

2. Where was Amos from and what was he doing when the word of the Lord came to him? (Amos 1:1)

3. What were some similarities, if any, of judgment against the nations, and what were some differences?

4. Why were the nations judged (Romans 2:14–15)? Why were Judah and Israel judged? (Deuteronomy 28:15–19; Amos 3:2)

5. What do you notice about the beginning of Amos 3:1, 4:1, and 5:1? What do you think Amos was trying to get across to them?

6. What did the Holy Spirit highlight to you in Amos 1—3 through the reading or the teaching?

Lesson 7: Amos 4—6

Restorer: Contending for the Faith

Teaching Notes

Intro

Remember Amos was from Tekoa, where he was most likely taking care of sheep. Amos was writing to the northern kingdom of Israel. Amos' words addressed two primary sins: the lack of true worship and the lack of justice. In the previous chapters, we have read about the judgment that the Israelites would experience.

Teaching

Amos 4:1–13: J. Vernon McGee wrote, "In verses 1–3 [Amos] directs his scathing judgment against the Northern Kingdom. In verses 4–5 [Amos], with biting sarcasm invited the people to transgress. They called it worship of the golden calf. In verses 6–13, [Amos pointed out that] they had been judged by scant harvests, plagues of insects, pestilences, war, and destruction. None of them had deterred them from sin."[1] I think it's fair to say that when weather or other troubles come into play, the Lord wants us to turn to Him. No matter what devastating things happened to the Israelites, they never cried out or returned to God.

Amos 5:1: Chapter five gives a description of the judgment the Israelites would discover. I would be kind of nervous to hear these judgments, after hearing a list of all the things I didn't do! The Israelites were having to face their consequences. This chapter starts out as a funeral dirge.

Amos 5:2–3: It's important to understand that as a young nation, God said to the Israelites, "I am cutting you off." The Israelites had taken God's gift of land and turned it into a place of death. MacArthur wrote, "Most [of the soldiers] were to be killed in battle or taken captive (a 90 percent casualty vote); only a handful would return."[2] This was not a good song.

---

[1] J. Vernon McGee, "Outline for Amos," https://www.blueletterbible.org/Comm/mcgee_j_vernon/notes-outlines/amos/amos-outline.cfm.

[2] John MacArthur, *The MacArthur Bible Commentary* (Nashville: Thomas Nelson, 2005), 997.

Amos 5:4–5: These verses were a praise to God. Amos' song began to change. "Seek Me and live!" is a much better song! Wiersbe writes, "To seek the Lord means first of all to change our thinking and abandon the vain thoughts that are directing our wayward lives."[3] Basically, to seek God is to pursue Him.

Amos wrote a warning to the Israelites to stay away from certain regions. People from the north had crossed over borders in order to worship false gods. Seek the Lord and have life. Wiersbe explains, "The prophet gave three reasons [to seek God], the first of which is that we might have life (v. 4) . . . The second reason we should seek God is because there is no other way to experience spiritual blessing (v. 5) . . . The third reason for seeking God is because judgment is coming (v. 6)."[4] The Israelites had not only failed to pursue God, they were pursuing false gods and idols.

Amos 5:6: A lot of people struggle with verse six where Amos wrote that God's judgment "would spread like fire throughout the house of Joseph." Fire was going to consume the house of Israel—everything. There are many evangelists and Christians that argue you shouldn't talk about hell when you share Jesus. This language that Amos used would be an incredibly helpful point for why people should trust Christ. Why should we trust Christ? Because we will experience eternal life and spiritual blessing through Him! There is no other way to experience God's goodness except through Christ. I have no problem saying, "If you don't trust Christ you are going to hell." That is the reality. Judgment is coming, if you don't seek God. Fire is coming. It is a unique foreshadowing of what is to come.

I think Amos' message to the Israelites is applicable to Christians today. God gave the Israelites (and us) multiple chances to seek Him and to pursue Him. We should constantly seek the Lord in everything. It doesn't have to be due to sin. It can come about through any decision in our lives.

Amos 5:7–8: MacArthur wrote, "Justice was so perverted that is was like wormwood, an herb known for its bitter taste (Revelation 8:11)."[5] The Israelites were taking things that were good and just and turning them bad. In verse 8, Amos mentioned Pleiades and Orion. MacArthur wrote, "Pleiades, part of the constellation Taurus, and Orion, depict God's creative power and wisdom. Israel was guilty of worshipping the stars instead of the creator."[6]

---

[3] Warren W. Wiersbe, *The Exposition Bible Commentary: Old Testament* (Colorado Springs: David C. Cook, 2002), 356.

[4] Wiersbe, 356–57.

[5] MacArthur, 997.

[6] MacArthur, 997.

Amos 5:10–13: God's judgment was coming, and the Israelites sought to avoid it. Anyone who spoke against them or spoke with integrity was disliked and rejected. Amos started to list many of the bad behaviors of the Israelites. These were habitual sins that Amos was pointing out. The days were so evil that Amos wrote that a wise person would keep silent.

Amos 5:14–15: Seek God; seek good. How much clearer could Amos be?

Amos 5:16–17: There would be mourning and wailing after God's judgment. MacArthur wrote, "At the Exodus, the Lord 'passed over' Israel; here He 'passes through,' much like He did to the Egyptians in Moses' day."[7] God was not sparing His people this time.

Amos 5:18–20: These are some pretty harsh words. God was done with the fakeness of their religion. MacArthur wrote, "Even the wicked wanted the Day of the Lord to come, mistakenly thinking that it would bring victory/blessing instead of certain judgment (Zephaniah 1:14–18)."[8]

Amos 5:21–24: The Israelites were going through the motions of worship. When done with the wrong heart, worship, sacrifices, and even sacred festivals displease the Lord.

Amos 5:25–27: Nelson's Commentary states, "After dismissing Israel's empty worship as noisy and tumultuous, God called for the rolling waters of justice and the perennial stream of righteousness, the only foundation for true praise and worship of the Lord."[9] This is a picture of what God wants.

Amos 6: McGee writes, "Israel was taking it easy, sitting in the lap of luxury in a day of affluence."[10] Throughout this chapter, Amos discussed the three national sins of the Israelites: gluttony, heathen music, and drunkenness. Amos pointed out how God hated the actions of the Israelites and that their actions would be punished. The chapter ends with another warning of the captivity to come to the nations.

---

[7] MacArthur, 997.

[8] MacArthur, 997.

[9] Earl D. Radmacher, Ronald B. Allen, and H. Wayne House, eds., *Nelson's New Illustrated Bible Commentary* (Nashville: Thomas Nelson, 1999), 1054.

[10] McGee.

Closing

God gave the Israelites multiple opportunities to seek Him. Even though this is ominous chapter in an already dark season, we can take hope and be thankful that God is the *Restorer* and He always looks to restore.

The Daily Word

Amos continued to speak to Israel, pointing out times the people did not return to the Lord. Over and over again, the people did not return to the Lord. God boldly, clearly, and simply spoke to the House of Israel: *Seek me and live. Seek Yahweh and live.* And yet what did the people continue to do? Walk away from the Lord.

The Lord desires an intimate relationship with you—His chosen, beloved people to whom He sent His Son, Jesus, to redeem. God commanded you to love Him above all else—with all your heart, soul, and mind. The Word of God states over and over: *Seek and you will find God. Draw near to God and He will draw near to you. Ask God and you will receive. Knock and the doors will be open. Seek first God's kingdom, and all things in life will be added to you.* God longs for you to pursue a relationship with Him. Pray, read His Word, have fellowship with other believers, and look for the Lord working in your life. When you seek Him, when you love Him with everything, *He will be found, and you will live.* He promises that as you seek Him, you will live abundantly in the love He desires to lavish on you.

For the LORD says to the house of Israel:
    Seek Me and live! —Amos 5:4

Questions

---

1. Who did Amos refer to and what did he mean when he used the phrase "cows of Bashan" in Amos 4:1? (Isaiah 3:16–26; 32:9–13; Jeremiah 4:30)

2. In Amos 4:4–5, what did Amos accuse them of while using sarcasm? How does the Lord feel about hypocrisy (Luke 6:46; 12:2; 1 Peter 2:16; 1 John 4:20)? Why would Amos tell them to do just the opposite in Amos 5:5?

3. What kind of message was given in Amos 5:1? What was the only way for Israel to live? (Amos 5:4, 6, 14)

4. What does it mean to hate evil and love good (Amos 5:15)? What did that look like for the Israelites? What does that look like for you today? (Psalm 119:163; Proverbs 6:16; 8:13; Isaiah 5:20; Mark 12:30; Romans 12:2, 9)

5. Why would the Lord not listen to the worship of the Israelites in Amos 5:23 (Leviticus 26:27, 31; Psalm 51:16–17, 19; 66:18)? When your heart or the heart of the Church is in sin, consider that this would be the Lord's response. How does this change how you approach God in worship?

6. What did the Holy Spirit highlight to you in Amos 4—6 through the reading or the teaching?

Lesson 8: Amos 7—9

Restorer: Amos' Visions

Teaching Notes

Intro

Today we wrap up our study of Amos, one of the minor prophets. The minor prophets were not designated "minor" because of a lack of importance but rather for their shorter length. Amos' message was for the ten tribes in the northern kingdom. In the southern kingdom were Judah, Benjamin and their capital, Jerusalem. Historically, both David and his son Solomon ruled over the united kingdoms, but after Solomon's forty-year reign, the united kingdoms were split into two.

The minor prophets spoke into these kingdoms as they moved further and further away from the Lord. The reality was that none of the people of either kingdom embraced the words of the minor and major prophets, which called them to return to God.

Amos 7—8 is a message of judgment. The word for the entire book of Amos that reflects Jesus is *Restorer*, and it is found at the very end of Amos.

Teaching

Amos 7–8: In chapter 7 God gave Amos a vision in which he watched something happen before him. The vision was a swarm of locusts from God, coming during the spring crop, that ate all the vegetation in the land. Amos understood that the locusts represented God's judgment and questioned how Jacob (meaning the northern kingdom) would survive. So, God agreed not to make the judgment happen (vv. 1–3).

God then gave Amos a second vision of fire that devoured the land. Again, Amos pleaded for the nation, and God relented of His coming judgment (vv. 4–6).

The third vision was then shown. God was holding a plumb line in his hand next to a vertical wall. God told Amos He would use the plumb line to judge His disobedient people (vv. 7–9). His judgment would come against the house of King Jeroboam.

When the priest Amaziah heard about Amos, he sent word of Amos' conspiracy against the king and the kingdom to Jeroboam. Amaziah also told Amos to go away to Judah and give his messages there. Amos replied that he spoke God's message to Israel as he had been called to do (vv. 10–16). Amos then prophesied that Amaziah's wife would become a prostitute, his sons and daughter would die, the land would be divided up, and Amaziah and others would be taken into exile (v. 17).

Amos 8:1–14: The fourth vision is in chapter 8. Amos saw a basket of summer fruit. Wiersbe explains, "Just as this fruit was ripe for eating, the nation of Israel was ripe for judgment."[1] God said the end had come for His people Israel (vv. 1–2). Verses 3–8 tell of the evils that Israel had committed. Therefore, God would turn their feasts into mourning, and they would all be in sackcloth in grief (v. 10). J. Vernon McGee summarizes verses 11–14 as "dark days would come."[2]

Amos 9:1–10: In his fifth vision, Amos saw the Lord standing beside the altar (v. 1a). This sounds like a hopeful statement, but the fifth vision was worse than the others. Verses 1–10 are about judgment and destruction. The temple would be destroyed, and the people would try unsuccessfully to escape. It didn't matter where they tried to hide. It didn't matter if they went to the depths of Sheol or the highest place in the universe, heaven. It didn't matter if they could go to Mount Carmel, the highest place in their area or to the sea floor, the lowest. God said He would command the sea serpent to bite them if they tried to hide on the sea floor. Even if they were taken into captivity, God would find them and pass judgment on them (vv. 1b–4). In Romans 8:38–39, Paul wrote that nothing could separate us from the love of God through Christ our Lord.

Amos described God's power—as creator, He can touch the earth and it will melt. MacArthur explains, "Like the Nile River, which annually provided water and rich soil deposits for farmers by greatly overflowing its banks, so judgment would overflow the land of Israel for the unrighteous arrogance of the nation."[3]

In verse 7 God told the Israelites they were the same as the Cushites, the Philistines, and the Arameans—other sinful nations. However, the judgment of the Israelites would not be as bad as it would be for those nations, because God would not totally destroy Israel. The eyes of the Lord were on the nation of Israel (v. 8). He was going to shake the house of Israel through other nations, but He would preserve a remnant of Israel (v. 9). Sadly, those who, in their

---

[1] Warren W. Wiersbe, *The Exposition Bible Commentary: Old Testament* (Colorado Springs: David C. Cook, 2002), 365.

[2] J. Vernon McGee, "Outline for Amos," https://www.blueletterbible.org/Comm/mcgee_j_vernon/notes-outlines/amos/amos-outline.cfm.

[3] John MacArthur, *The MacArthur Bible Commentary* (Nashville: Thomas Nelson, 2005), 999; see note for Amos 8:8.

ignorance and sin, thought they could never face disaster would die by the sword (v. 10).

Amos 9:11–15: However, despite the dire warnings, there was hope in Amos' message. There will be a remnant from David that will be restored (v. 11). The land would be rebuilt, and the remnant would be given power over the nations that defeated Israel. The Lord would make all this happen (v. 12).

Verse 13 begins a picture of prosperity. The plowmen, those who tread grapes, and those who sowed seeds will be back at work. The mountains and hills will flow with produced wine. The fortunes of the people will be restored, and they will rebuild their cities, vineyards, and gardens (v. 14). God promised He would plant the remnant on their land, and they would never be uprooted again (v. 15).

Verses 11–15 are a picture of the millennial kingdom to come. When Jesus comes back the second time, after the seven years of tribulation, He will usher in a thousand-year reign. That reign is what is described in these verses.

Closing

Amos goes from judgment to restoration. When Christ returns, He will plant the Jews back in their land. They will never again be uprooted because Jesus is the ultimate *Restorer*.

The Daily Word

As Amos walked obediently with the Lord, proclaiming messages to Israel, he faced opposition from Amaziah. Amos' role as prophet for the Lord may not have made sense to others because he worked as a herdsman and didn't come from a family heritage of prophets. However, Amos stood confidently in his calling and continued receiving visions and proclaiming the messages from the Lord.

Has the Lord called you into something? Perhaps you work at a factory or are an elementary teacher. Maybe you are even retired. And yet the Lord has called you to teach and proclaim His Word to this next generation. You may question this calling because you don't come from a family of pastors or haven't been to seminary. Even so, remember, *when the Lord calls you into something, He will provide.* He will guide you. He will strengthen you. Beware of opposition from the world and lies from the enemy. Stand firm as a child of God and follower of Christ. He will be your confidence and keep your foot from slipping. He who calls you is faithful and will always be faithful.

So Amos answered Amaziah, "I was not a prophet or the son of a prophet; rather, I was a herdsman, and I took care of sycamore figs. But the Lord took

me from following the flock and said to me: 'Go, prophesy to My people Israel.'" —Amos 7:14–15

Further Scripture: Proverbs 3:26; John 15:16; 1 Thessalonians 5:24

Questions

1. How did Amos intercede for the people when God showed him the first vision (Amos 7:1–3)? What other characters in Scripture also interceded for the people? (Genesis 18:22–32; Exodus 32:30–32; Romans 9:1–3)

2. What were the five visions the Lord gave Amos? (Amos 7:1–9, 8:1–3, 9:1–6)

3. Why do you think Amos interceded for the people on the first two visions but did not intercede for them on the last three? (Jeremiah 7:16; 11:14; 14:11)

4. How did the priest Amaziah react to Amos' prophecy (Amos 7:10–13)? What did Amos recognize about his calling from God?

5. How did the Lord encourage Amos after both a hard encounter with Amaziah and giving him tough visions to speak (Amos 9:11–15)? How did God encourage some others in Scripture after going through tough times (Acts 18:9–11; 27:21–26; 2 Timothy 4:16–17)? Think of a time when the Lord encouraged you while going through something hard or coming out of it.

6. What did the Holy Spirit highlight to you in Amos 7—9 through the reading or the teaching?

Lesson 9: Obadiah

Established King: Judgment on Edom and Others

Teaching Notes

Intro

So far in our study of the twelve minor prophets, we've studied Hosea, Joel, and Amos. Today, we move to the short book of Obadiah. All of the minor prophets, as well as the major prophets, led up to either the Assyrian or the Babylonian captivity. All the prophets also had messages either for the northern kingdom of Israel or the southern kingdom of Judah. They all pronounced that judgment was coming either through the Assyrian or the Babylonian armies. Obadiah's message, however, was unique from all the other prophets.

Obadiah's name means "servant of the Lord." The book of Obadiah is the shortest book in the Old Testament. There's only one chapter in the book. Nothing is known about the prophet Obadiah. The name is mentioned eleven times in the Old Testament but does not appear to be referring to the prophet. Some scholars believe Obadiah was actually part of the southern kingdom of Judah because he frequently mentioned Judah, Jerusalem, and Zion.

Scholars suggest Obadiah was a contemporary of Elijah and Elisha. MacArthur explains, "The date of writing is equally difficult to determine, though it is associated with the Edomite assault on Jerusalem described in verses 10–14."[1] There were actually four invasions against Jerusalem during the Old Testament, and Obadiah wrote after one of them. MacArthur outlines these invasions: "(1) by Shishak, king of Egypt, c. 925 BC, during the reign of Rehoboam (1 Kings 14:25, 26; 2 Chronicles 12); (2) by the Philistines and Arabians between 848–841 BC during the reign of Jehoram of Judah (2 Chronicles 21:8–20; (3) by Jehoash, king of Israel, c. 790 BC (2 Kings 14; 2 Chronicles 25); and (4) by Nebuchadnezzar, king of Babylon, in the fall of Jerusalem in 586 BC."[2] MacArthur states that, based on historical evidence,

---

[1] John MacArthur, *The MacArthur Bible Commentary* (Nashville: Thomas Nelson, 2005), 1001.

[2] MacArthur, 1001.

only the second and fourth invasions are real possibilities, but that the second invasion seems preferable because of the information provided in verse 1.[3]

The Edomites descended from Esau, the eldest son of Isaac and Rebekah (Genesis 25:24–26). Esau was the twin brother of Jacob and wrestled with Jacob in the womb (Genesis 25:22). The brothers never got along, and Jacob tricked Esau into selling his birthright as the firstborn to him. The name of Esau means "hairy" because "he was like a hairy garment all over" (NKJV). Esau was also called Edom, which means "red" because he sold his birthright for "red stew" (Genesis 25:30).[4] Jacob was also known as Israel.

Esau broke the covenant agreement with the Lord and married two Canaanite women and then the daughter of Ishmael (Genesis 26:34, 28:9). Esau did everything he could to go against the lineage God had blessed: Abraham, Isaac, and then Jacob. From the time they were small boys, Esau preferred to be outside as a hunter while Jacob preferred to stay home (Genesis 25:27). Esau settled in a mountainous area, which was located south of the Dead Sea. Jacob settled in the good land. These two boys led to nations that were enemies against each other which was foretold (Genesis 25:23).[5] Clearly God's hand was on Jacob and Israel, and God was against Esau and Edom.

Teaching

Obadiah 1–9: In verse 1 God proclaimed a word about Edom and said He had sent a messenger among the nations to rise up against Edom. God said He would make the nation of Edom insignificant to all other nations, and they would be greatly despised (v. 2). God said the Edomites had a false sense of security from living in caves where they felt they were untouchable (v. 3). While it would be difficult for man to get to the Edomites, God could bring them down (v. 4). God said that even if the Edomites made their home on the stars, He would still bring them down through His judgment. Not only would Edom be brought down, but all the wealth they had been so proud of would be plundered (vv. 5–6). According to Wiersbe, "The Lord would work so that their alliances would be broken (v. 7)."[6]

"In that day" God promised to also destroy Edom's wisdom (v. 8). Wiersbe explains, "The people of the east were known for their wisdom (1 Kings 4:30), and this included the Edomites . . . Job's friend Eliphaz was from Teman in Edom (Job 2:11; Jeremiah 49:7). Without wisdom, the leaders of Edom couldn't make

---

[3] MacArthur, 1001.

[4] MacArthur, 1001.

[5] MacArthur, 1001.

[6] Warren W. Wiersbe, *The Exposition Bible Commentary: Old Testament* (Colorado Springs: David C. Cook, 2002), 373.

the right decisions, and the result would be confusion."[7] Teman was the grandson of Esau, and the army of Teman would be destroyed (v. 9).

Obadiah 10–14: Edom would be covered with shame and destroyed forever because of their violence toward Jacob/Israel (v. 10). Notice there was no promise to Edom that a remnant would survive. In verse 11, God outlined the sins of Edom against Judah—they stood and watched as Israel was captured and the holy city of Jerusalem was plundered. They assisted those who had invaded Jerusalem and even rejoiced over Judah's fall (v. 12). Edom also plundered the city and helped bring about their downfall. They even prevented the fugitives from escaping captivity (vv. 13–14).

Obadiah 15–18: God said "the Day of the Lord" when Christ returns is near, and He would come against all the nations that turned against Israel. What the nations had done against Israel would be done to them (v. 15). Edom was an example for all the other nations of what would happen to them if they mistreated Israel. They would experience the cup of God's wrath, and it would be like they had never existed (v. 16). Mount Zion would be delivered and made holy again (v. 17). The houses of Jacob and Joseph will become blazing flames that will turn the other nations into stubble (v. 18). There will be no survivors left of those who had stood against Israel.

Obadiah 19–21: The Jews will be restored to the land that had been given to them originally (vv. 19–20). "Saviors" will be on Mount Zion to rule, but the kingdom will belong to God (v. 21). The term "saviors" can be understood as "deliverers." Wiersbe explains, "King Messiah will have 'deliverers' assist Him in His rule over the nations."[8]

Closing

Obadiah points us to the setting up of the millennial kingdom. Revelation 11:15 says, "The seventh angel blew his trumpet, and there were loud voices in heaven saying: The kingdom of the world has become the kingdom of our Lord and of His Messiah, and He will reign forever and ever!"

---

[7] Wiersbe, 375.

[8] Wiersbe, 375.

The Daily Word

The Lord called Obadiah to proclaim a prophetic message to the country of Edom—*You will be covered in shame and destroyed forever because of the violence done to Israel.* The Lord's message through Obadiah communicated that all nations who brought opposition to Israel would suffer the Lord's judgment. Why does this judgment against other nations take place? Because God's covenant with Israel will always prevail.

The book of Obadiah warns of the wrath of God, but it also reminds you to *celebrate the love of God.* Yes! The Day of the Lord is coming. Christ will return and ascend Mount Zion to rule overall. As you anticipate His glorious return, open your eyes to see people around you. When you see others struggling in their faith or in a season of destruction, don't be like the Edomites and mock them, rejoicing in their misfortunes and gloating in their miseries. Rather, as God's chosen instrument, *be a vessel of His love*, showing mercy, kindness, and gentleness. In this way, when Christ returns, *people will be ready. You will be ready.* And, Lord willing, all people will know of His faithful love and mercy.

For the Day of the Lord is near,
against all the nations.
As you have done, so it will be done to you;
what you deserve will return on your own head. —Obadiah 15

Further Scripture: Psalm 145:8; Acts 9:15; Revelation 11:15

Questions

1. How did Obadiah receive his message from the Lord? Who was the vision about?

2. From whom did the Edomites descend (Genesis 25:24–26; 36:8)? What was the background of Jacob and Esau? How was Esau disobedient to God? (Genesis 25:22, 25, 27, 30; 26:34; 27:38–40; 28:9)

3. What would you say was the defining characteristic of Edom (Jeremiah 49:16; Obadiah 3)? What follows an arrogant or prideful heart (Proverb 11:2; 16:18; Ezekiel 7:10–12)? How does God speak about the proud? (Luke 14:11; James 4:6)

4. What sins had Edom committed? (Obadiah 10–16)

5. What three promises did God give to His own people? (Obadiah 17–18, 19–20, 21)

6. What did the Holy Spirit highlight to you in Obadiah through the reading or the teaching?

Lesson 10: Jonah 1—4

Resurrection: Jonah's Preaching

Teaching Notes

Intro

While the minor prophets' writings are shorter than the major prophets, the minor prophets have powerful messages. Jonah is one of the better-known minor prophets, and his book contains a lot of valuable insight for us. All of us have probably felt like Jonah at some point.

Jonah's name means "dove." In Jonah's case, he was a dove that flew away and refused to be obedient to its master at the beginning of the book. Throughout the book, Jonah referred to himself in the third person. MacArthur shares this practice was not uncommon in the Old Testament.[1]

Jonah was mentioned in 2 Kings 14:25: "He restored Israel's border from Lebo-hamath as far as the Sea of the Arabah, according to the word of the LORD, the God of Israel, had spoken through His servant, the prophet Jonah son of Amittai from Gath-hepher." Gath-hepher was near Nazareth and was established during the reign of Jeroboam II from 793–753 BC. According to MacArthur, Jonah would have been a prophet to the northern tribe of Israel just prior to Amos coming on to the scene. Jewish tradition holds that Jonah was the son of the widow of Zarephath that Elijah raised from the dead (1 Kings 17).[2]

During Jonah's ministry, Syria and Assyria were relatively weak, which allowed Jeroboam II to expand the borders of Israel to where they had been during David's reign. This was a time of peace and prosperity in the kingdom. However, the people were in spiritual poverty. MacArthur observed: "Religion was ritualistic and increasingly idolatrous, and justice had become perverted. . . . As a result, God was to punish her by bringing destruction and captivity from the Assyrians in 722 BC."[3] Jonah can be considered the first part of a larger story with Nahum serving as the second part.[4]

---

[1] John MacArthur, *The MacArthur Bible Commentary* (Nashville: Thomas Nelson, 2005), 1006.

[2] MacArthur, 1006.

[3] MacArthur, 1007.

[4] MacArthur, 1008.

Eventually in Jonah, we will see Nineveh repent of its sin after Jonah was obedient to God's command. Because of the success of his ministry in Nineveh, Jonah is not remembered primarily as a prophet of Israel. Nineveh was the capital of Assyria. As MacArthur observed, Nineveh was "infamous for its cruelty" and was a "historical nemesis of Israel and Judah." Nineveh had been founded by Nimrod, the grandson of Noah, and was possibly the largest city in the ancient world.[5]

Teaching

Jonah 1:1–12: God commanded Jonah to go to Nineveh and "preach against it" (vv. 1–2). Jonah knew that the Ninevites might repent if he went and preached to them, so he "got up to flee to Tarshish from the LORD's presence" (v. 3). Jonah paid to sail on a boat, away from God's commandment to preach to Nineveh. The text makes it clear, that Jonah did so to flee "from the LORD's presence," by using the phrase twice in verse 3.

MacArthur notes four divisions of Jonah's story in chapter 1:

1. "The Commission of Jonah (1:1–2)"
2. "The Flight of Jonah (1:3)"
3. "The Pursuit of Jonah (1:4–16)"—Jonah fell asleep on the boat. A storm began to rage on the sea. Jonah confessed to the sailors that the storm was because of his disobedience to God and told them to throw him overboard.
4. "The Preservation of Jonah (1:17)"[6]—Jonah was swallowed by a "huge fish" and was in its belly for three days and three nights.

Jonah 2: MacArthur observed Jonah "Submitting to God's will" in chapter 2 in four stages:

1. "The Helplessness of Jonah (2:1–3)"
2. "The Prayer of Jonah (2:4–7)"
3. "The Repentance of Jonah (2:8–9)" Jonah finally acknowledged his need for the Lord and his commitment to Him.
4. "The Deliverance of Jonah (2:10)."[7]

Jonah 3: After Jonah submitted to God's will, he was given a second chance to be obedient by preaching to Nineveh (vv. 1–3). Jonah had to travel 500 miles from

---

[5] MacArthur, 1007.

[6] MacArthur, 1008–10.

[7] MacArthur, 1011.

Joppa just to get to Nineveh. Nineveh itself was so large it took three days just to walk around the entire city. Jonah proclaimed that Nineveh would be destroyed in 40 days. The people of Nineveh believed the obedient prophet as he proclaimed God's message, proclaimed a fast, and dressed in sackcloth in repentance (v. 5).

Jesus used the Ninevites' response to Jonah's message as a critique of his generation: "But He answered them, 'An evil and adulterous generation demands a sign, but no sign will be given to it except the sign of the prophet Jonah. For as Jonah was in the belly of the huge fish three days and nights, so the Son of Man will be in the heart of the earth three days and three nights. The men of Nineveh will stand up at the judgment with this generation and condemn it, because they repented at Jonah's proclamation; and look—something greater than Jonah is here!'" (Matthew 12:39–41). Jesus used Jonah's time in the belly of the fish as a way to prophesy that He would rise from the dead. That's why our word for Jonah is *Resurrection*. "Jesus said to her, 'I am the resurrection and the life. The one who believes in Me, even if he dies, will live'" (John 11:25). The message of the book of Jonah preaches the gospel.

Nineveh's repentance was so thorough that even the king "took off his royal robe, put on sackcloth, and sat in ashes." (v. 6) He issued a decree that everyone, including animals, was to fast from food and water. God gave Jonah a second chance after Jonah messed up, and God used Him to lead a great city to repentance. The Ninevites "turned from their evil ways—so God relented from the disaster He had threatened to do to them" (v. 10).

Jonah 4: The Ninevites' repentance "greatly displeased" Jonah (v. 1). After Jonah performed the Lord's will, he began to question whether or not he had done God's will. Jonah was then rebuked by the Lord (vv. 6–11). God cared about the Ninevites and desired their repentance.

Closing

Jonah reveals the gospel. Lemuel Young highlighted six ways Jonah reveals the gospel:

1. "Like Jonah, our sin separates us from God's presence."
2. "A life of sin brings storms that are too great for us to handle."
3. "The domino effect."—Our sin impacts others. Jonah's sin caused problems for the sailors on the ship.
4. "The story of Jonah shows the love of God."
5. "Jesus is greater than Jonah."
6. "Faith comes from hearing the Word of God."[8]

---

[8] Lemuel Young, "6 Ways Jonah Reveals the Gospel," https://www.grace.one/blog/6-ways-jonah-reveals-the-gospel.

The Daily Word

The Lord called Jonah to proclaim His message to the people of Nineveh. But Jonah fled and ran away from his call. Consequently, the Lord allowed storms in Jonah's life, even putting him in the belly of a whale until Jonah submitted to the will of the Lord. As Jonah preached in Nineveh, the people turned from their evil ways and sought the Lord. Jonah was angered by the Lord's mercy for Nineveh, and he questioned God's will. In response, God rebuked Jonah.

You may relate with some or even all of Jonah's story: running away from God's will, facing storms in life, faithfully walking out God's call, experiencing God moving powerfully, seeing God shine through people around you, questioning God's will, or getting rebuked by God. No matter where you are, *God is with you, He is sovereign, and He is working*. He is strength in your weakness. Today, have faith to believe in Jesus and trust He is working through every season of your life. Seek Him, fix your eyes on Him, and trust Him, even when you can't see it. He Is with you. Yes, He is with you.

As my life was fading away
I remembered Yahweh.
My prayer came to You,
to Your holy temple.
Those who cling to worthless idols
forsake faithful love,
but as for me, I will sacrifice to You
with a voice of thanksgiving.
I will fulfill what I have vowed.
Salvation is from the Lord! —Jonah 2:7–9

Further Scripture: Matthew 12:39–41; Luke 11:30; Romans 10:9–10

Questions

1. According to Jonah 1:4–5, Jonah was asleep on a ship below the deck while a great storm raged. How does this parallel with the Messiah in Matthew 8:24–25?

2. Some details in Matthew can be reflective of parts of Jonah. But how do the words of the men on the ship in Jonah 1:14 differ from the words of the crowd in Matthew 27:25?

3. How long was Jonah in the belly of the great fish (Jonah 1:17)? How does this point to the Messiah? (Matthew 12:40)

4. What part of Jonah's prayer in chapter 2 points to the Messiah? (Psalm 16:10; 103:4; Jonah 2:2, 4; Matthew 28:6)

5. Jonah knew (Jonah 4:2) that if the Lord saw repentance in Nineveh, He would relent from the calamity He sent Jonah to declare to them (Exodus 34:6; Numbers 14:18; Nehemiah 9:31; Psalm 86:5, 15; 103:8; 145:8). Did the Lord desire this kind of response from Israel and Judah when He brought warnings of calamity to them (2 Chronicles 7:13–14; Isaiah 30:15, 18; Jeremiah 18:5–11)? Why do you think Nineveh repented but the Lord's people did not?

6. What did the Holy Spirit highlight to you in Jonah 1—4 through the reading or the teaching?

Lesson 11: Micah 1—3

The Shepherd: God's Word Was Rejected

Teaching Notes

Intro

Last week, in our discussion of the minor prophets, we covered Hosea, Joel, and part of Amos. This week, we've finished the book of Amos, as well as Obadiah, and Jonah. Today we continue our study with the book of Micah. Mindi's painting for Micah is one of my favorites. From Micah 5:4, we get the one word that describes Jesus in this book: *The Shepherd* who reigns. The name Micah means "who is like the Lord?" Micah is the shortened version of the name Micaiah or Michaiah.[1] Basically, Micah received a word from the Lord and was commissioned to proclaim it. In Micah 2, he talks about the sins of Judah. We've talked before about the fact that the prophets' messages were not well received because of the oracles, woes, and judgments in them. But then there was this little bit of hope offered.

According to Micah 1:1, Micah was a Moreshite. We know nothing of his parents. He was from Moresheth, located in the foothills of Judah about 25 miles southwest of Jerusalem, near Gath in Philistia.[2] The northern kingdom would fall to Assyria during Micah's ministry. Though Micah dated his ministry with references to the kings of Judah, on occasion, his words were for Israel (the northern kingdom). But overall, his primary focus was the southern kingdom of Judah where he lived. Historically, these were days of economic prosperity and no violence—so things were good. But things were beginning to slip. Syria and Israel invaded Judah and temporarily took wicked Ahaz captive. After Assyria overthrew Syria and Israel, Hezekiah, the good king of Judah, withdrew his allegiance from Assyria. This caused Sennacherib to attack Jerusalem in 701 BC. In 2 Chronicles 32:21, God sent His angel to deliver Judah. God then used Hezekiah to lead Judah back to worshiping the Lord.[3] MacArthur explains, "After the prosperous reign of Uzziah, who died in 739 BC, his son Jotham continued

---

[1] John MacArthur, *The MacArthur Bible Commentary* (Nashville: Thomas Nelson, 2005), 1014.

[2] MacArthur, 1014.

[3] MacArthur, 1014.

the same policies, but failed to remove the centers of idolatry."[4] Judah's outward prosperity became fake; their idolatry with Baal, the Canaanite fertility god, was integrated with their Old Testament sacrificial system. So, as Amos had spoken into Israel, Micah began to speak into Judah.[5]

Micah began to proclaim a message of judgment to people who were persistently pursuing evil. In Micah 1:2 and 6:1–2, Micah used imagery almost like a courtroom mentality. Micah portrayed his message like a courtroom with Judah on trial. There are three oracles or warnings in the book of Micah. The command to "listen" was used in each (Micah 1:2; 3:1; 6:1). With each command to listen Micah moves from doom to hope. Each of the three sections includes the sins of the people, the punishment of God to come, and then the promises of hope for the faithful after the judgment.[6]

Teaching

Micah 1:1–7: The prophecy was against Samaria, which then reached Jerusalem. Samaria was the capital of the northern kingdom, where a golden calf was worshipped. According to verse 2, God was going to bring judgment against Samaria. The Assyrians would be used as God's instrument to judge Samaria. Many scholars believe verse 4 describes events that will happen much later—at the return of Christ's coming in judgment. Jerusalem had become a place of heathen worship and would receive God's judgment (v. 5). Verses 6–7 describe the coming judgment. Destruction did come to Samaria through the Assyrians in 722 BC. Then destruction of Jerusalem came through Babylon in 586 BC. But many scholars believe this also refers to the judgment that will occur when Christ comes back and judges His people and the other nations.

Micah 1:8–16: These verses contain Micah's lamentation. As a prophet releasing this word from God, it did not bring Micah joy. He was not excited about what would happen to his people and his city. Micah lamented what would happen to the cities of Gath ("weep town"), Beth-leaphrah ("dust town"), Shaphir ("beauty town"), Zaanan ("march town"), Maroth ("bitterness"), Lachish ("horse town"), and Achzib ("lie town").[7]

Micah 2:1–11: Micah began to describe the woes that would come upon his people, specifically the sins of the wealthy. They dreamed up wickedness and then

---

[4] MacArthur, 1014.

[5] MacArthur, 1014–15.

[6] MacArthur, 1015.

[7] J. Vernon McGee, *Jonah and Micah*, Thru the Bible Commentary Series (Nashville: Thomas Nelson, 1991), n. p.

did it (v. 1), taking the fields, houses, and inheritances of others (v. 2). Therefore, God planned disaster for the nation (vv. 3–5). Once the prophet released the word, the false prophets entered into the picture. "Quit your preaching," they said (v. 6). Instead of listening to Micah, the false prophets communicated a false message of prosperity. However, God's Word is revealed by those who obey Him and will be rejected by those who don't obey Him. The message of false prophets will be inconsistent with the message of the Holy Spirit. God called out those who oppressed the poor and took advantage of widows (vv. 8–9). For these reasons, God would deliver them to destruction (v. 10).

Micah 2:12–13: Remember how, in the midst of destruction, there's always this little bit of hope? God promised to gather the remnant of those who were faithful to Him. *The Shepherd* would gather His sheep and care for them in the fold. Jesus is the good shepherd who gathers His people. In John 10:11, Jesus said, "I am the good shepherd. The good shepherd lays down his life for the sheep." Jesus knows His sheep, and they know Him (John 10:14). Micah 4:7–8 is another passage that describes this remnant mentality. This picture only takes place when Christ comes to rule in the millennium. Micah 5:7–8 says the same thing. God, as a shepherd, says that even though judgment is coming against Judah for their sins, He will still gather His people. The remnant is essential in the book of Micah. God doesn't hold onto His anger forever; He delights in faithful love. God wants the faithful to be part of the remnant because He is patient and loving.

To the word remnant, you have to add the word "regathering." Though they were scattered all over the place, God began to gather the faithful back into His fold. Verse 13 portrays the image of *The Shepherd* and king who will be their leader. All of this will take place in the millennium. *The Shepherd* will gather the flock, but the King will rule over them as King of kings and Lord of lords. John MacArthur said the remnant is "a small nucleus of God's people, preserved by His sovereign grace, form this righteous remnant in the midst of a national apostasy."[8]

Closing

God always finds the few that are obedient; those who have persevered, obeyed, and looked to Him. *The Shepherd* is always looking for His remnant.

The Daily Word

The Lord called upon the prophet Micah to declare truth to Israel. The Lord continued to appear to Israel even though *Israel remained in rebellion*. Micah stood apart from the false prophets because the Spirit of the Lord filled him with

---

[8] MacArthur, 772.

power, justice, and the courage to proclaim truth to Israel about their sin and rebellion. Yet even with the strong message of justice, warning, and destruction, Micah offered the hope and deliverance of God *as their great Shepherd who would gather and lead His remnant.* The Lord will know them by name, and they will know His voice.

Dear friends, the Holy Spirit equips you, empowers you, and guides you. He will fill you with joy and peace so that you overflow with hope. The Lord longs to guide you as your Shepherd. *He sees your rebellion and your wandering ways, He knows your heart, and He longs to have you safe in His arms.* The Lord will equip you with authority in His name to do His work. You don't have to walk out your calling, doing the will of your heavenly Father in your own strength. *You are not alone.* The Holy Spirit's power speaks through you, counseling you, leading you, and guiding you. Today, call upon the name of the Lord, and He will be your strength.

As for me, however, I am filled with power
by the Spirit of the Lord,
with justice and courage,
to proclaim to Jacob his rebellion
and to Israel his sin. —Micah 3:8

Further Scripture: Micah 2:12; John 10:11; Romans 15:13

Questions

1. In Micah 2:13, the "One who breaks open the way" will go before them. Do you think this could be a reference to the Messiah? Why?

2. Micah 3:2–4 describes the leaders as devouring the flesh and tearing off the skin of those they lead. What was the role of the leaders supposed to be regarding the people? Read Galatians 5:15. The early church seemed to be dealing with a similar problem. Do you think this biting and consuming one another still happens in the church today? If so, what does it look like?

3. What do you think Micah meant when he said to the prophets that it would be night and darkness for them (Micah 3:6)?

4. What did the Holy Spirit highlight to you in Micah 1—3 through the reading or the teaching?

Lesson 12: Micah 4—5

The Shepherd: From Defeated Ruler to
Conquering King

Teaching Notes

Intro

The minor prophets are shorter books, but they contain a lot of meat. In Micah, the picture of Jesus is *The Shepherd*. The book of Micah has three oracles of warning. The third is in Micah 3 and talks about the leadership of the country. Micah 3:1–4 talks about the sins of the princes. Micah 3:5–8 talks about the sins of the false teachers and the judgment they will face. In Micah 3:9–12, the destruction of Jerusalem is covered because of the sins of the nation.

Teaching

Micah 4:1–13: J. Vernon McGee summarizes Micah 4 as "a prediction of the millennial kingdom, with Jerusalem as the center of worship and government. At that time swords will be beaten into plowshares (v. 3)."[1] This means that war will be no more and there will be a period of peace and prosperity. Joel 3:9–10 describes it as a holy war. The people will find peace and security in their own vineyards and gardens (vv. 4–5) (Zechariah 3:10). Jesus, *The Shepherd*, will gather the people who have been scattered, into His kingdom (vv. 7–8) (John 10:10).

In verses 9 through Micah 5:1, their future captivity was announced. Constable explains, "The Israelites would leave Jerusalem as a woman in labor."[2] However, the Lord would rescue them in Babylon and deliver them from captivity (v.10). Verses 11–13 give a picture of the coming battle in Armageddon.

Micah 5:1–9: Micah 5 continues the same timeline as Micah 4. Verse 1 actually belongs with chapter 4. Most likely, verse 1 is "a reference to the capture of King

---

[1] J. Vernon McGee, "Outline for Micah," https://www.blueletterbible.org/Comm/mcgee_j_vernon/notes-outlines/micah/micah-outline.cfm.

[2] Thomas L. Constable, *Expository Notes of Dr. Thomas Constable: Micah*, 43, https://planobiblechapel.org/tcon/notes/pdf/micah.pdf.

Zedekiah at the hands of Babylon in 586 BC"[3] (2 Kings 24–25). Verse 2 is a prophetic verse about Jesus: "Bethlehem Ephrathah, you are small among the clans of Judah; One will come from you to be the ruler over Israel for Me. His origin is from antiquity, from eternity." This describes the first advent coming of Christ. In Matthew 2:1–2, the wise men knew the prophecy of Micah 5:2. They expected Him to be born in Bethlehem, and they knew He came as king. McGee writes, "In His humanity Christ came from Bethlehem. In His deity, Christ came from eternity" (Matthew 2:5–6).[4]

Verse 3 points to the time we are currently in—when Jesus has been born through the first advent but has not returned for the second. MacArthur describes this as "the times of the Gentiles when Israel rejects Christ and is under the domination of enemies."[5] The second advent is referred to in the statement, "Then the rest of His brothers will return to the people of Israel." Christ will come back to gather and shepherd His brothers in the majestic name of Yahweh His God (v. 4). This points to the millennial rule of Christ. In verse 5 the Isaiah 9:6 picture is echoed—"He will be their peace."

MacArthur describes the tension in verses 7–9: "Israel's presence in the midst of many peoples would be to some a source of blessing; to others, she would be like a lion—a source of fear and destruction."[6] The remnant of Jacob will truly be blessed, and their enemies will be destroyed.

Micah 5:10–15: Constable describes verses 10–15 as "the purification of Zion."[7] Constable explains, "In that future eschatological day, the Lord also promised to remove the vain sources of security that had always tempted the Israelites, represented by: 'horses,' 'chariots,' 'cities,' and 'fortifications.'"[8] God would also remove altars to false gods, carved images, and the Asherah poles, sorcerers, and fortune-tellers (10–14). God also promised to take vengeance against the nations that had not obeyed Him.

Closing

Finally, after Micah 4 and the end of Micah 5, we have a message of incredible hope. Micah 4 draws the picture of what the millennial kingdom will look like. Micah 5 adds color and details to that description. The message for both chapters is to get ready because Jesus the Messiah is coming back.

---

[3] John MacArthur, *The MacArthur Bible Commentary* (Nashville: Thomas Nelson, 2005), 1019.

[4] McGee.

[5] MacArthur, 1019.

[6] MacArthur, 1019.

[7] Constable, 52.

[8] Constable, 52.

For the Gentiles, the message is to embrace Jesus the Messiah.

For the Jews, the message is similar but includes more. Scripture says there is a partial hardening among the Jews that will last until all the Gentiles have had the chance to hear about Jesus. There are currently 196 countries that have not heard about Jesus. The gospel has to go into those lands before the end times will be put in motion. Only then will the world face the Great Tribulation. Somewhere in that process, the Jewish people will become ready to accept Jesus as their Messiah.

2 Peter 3:10—13 states:

> But the Day of the Lord will come like a thief; on that day the heavens will pass away with a loud noise, the elements will burn and be dissolved, and the earth and the works on it will be disclosed. Since all these things are to be destroyed in this way, it is clear what sort of people you should be in holy conduct and godliness as you wait for and earnestly desire the coming of the day of God. The heavens will be on fire and be dissolved because of it, and the elements will melt with the heat. But based on His promise, we wait for the new heavens and a new earth, where righteousness will dwell.

The Daily Word

After the Babylonian exile, God promised to restore His people to Jerusalem. *Micah prophetically proclaimed of the coming King* from the line of Judah who would be born to rule over Israel. Indeed Jesus, God's Son, would be born in Bethlehem and shepherd the people of Israel. And then, after a time, Jesus would return in the strength of Yahweh and in the majestic name of Yahweh His God. All people who call upon His name will live securely in His greatness extending to the ends of the earth. Yes, *Jesus will be peace to all people*. He will reign from antiquity to eternity.

Jesus is both the Great Shepherd and the King of kings. He was born to redeem an entire world, offering hope and restoration to His people. He is your peace, your strength, and your security. Are your eyes focused on the world—on false gods, other forms of security, prized earthly possessions, or rich food and drink? Like He did with the Israelites, the Lord promises to remove things from your life that distract your vision and ability to fix your eyes on Jesus alone. He is the *only* peace. He is the *only* security. Today, give thanks for the birth of the Son given to the world named Wonderful Counselor, Mighty God, Eternal Father, Prince of Peace.

He will stand and shepherd them
in the strength of Yahweh,
in the majestic name of Yahweh His God.
They will live securely,
for then His greatness will extend
to the ends of the earth.
He will be their peace. —Micah 5:4–5

Further Scripture: Isaiah 9:6; Micah 5:2; Matthew 2:4–6

Questions

1. What and when was Micah 4:1–8 speaking about? (Isaiah 2:3–5; Acts 1:6–8; Revelation 21)

2. Who was Micah 5:2 talking about (Luke 2:11)? Who were some of the other prophets that prophesied Jesus' coming to earth to live as a man? (Isaiah 53; Jeremiah 30:21–22; 33:14–16; Zechariah 9:9)

3. Micah 5:5–15 speaks of the coming judgment on Israel's enemies. Does this scare you considering how many countries have turned their backs on Israel?

4. What did the Holy Spirit highlight to you in Micah 4—5 through the reading or the teaching?

Lesson 13: Micah 6—7

The Shepherd: Judgment and Restoration

Teaching Notes

Intro

Minor prophets have big messages, but they don't take all day to talk about them. Their books are much shorter than the major prophets, but their messages are still important and big. "Micah" is short for Micaiah or Michaiah. Micah prophesied to the southern tribes (Judah) of Israel. One of the themes of today's chapters will be the restoration of the united kingdom. While Micah prophesied about the destruction of the northern kingdom, he warned the southern kingdom that they faced God's judgment too.[1]

Teaching

Micah 6:1–16: Micah's language resembles a lawyer's. He wrote that the Lord had a "lawsuit" and a "case" to bring before the people (v. 2). When the Lord has a case against His people, things are not going well. The Lord's case against His people was so important that the Lord Himself would argue against Judah (v. 2). God challenged the people to bring their case against Him to inform Him of "how have I wearied you?" (v. 3). God reminded His people of how He had redeemed them (v. 4) and how He had not allowed Balaam to curse His people (v. 5).

God then questioned what His people should have done in response to the goodness He had shown them. He listed a variety of offerings that the people may have brought in response to His kindness to them (vv. 6–7). Instead of offerings or the external motions of religion, God wanted His people "to act justly, to love faithfulness, and to walk humbly with your God" (v. 8).

God was more concerned with the heart condition of His people than with the religious practices they engaged in. Matthew 7:21–23 states, "Not everyone who says to Me, 'Lord, Lord!' will enter the kingdom of heaven, but only the one who does the will of My Father in heaven. On that day many will say to Me, 'Lord, Lord, didn't we prophesy in Your name, drive out demons in Your name,

---

[1] Thomas L. Constable, *Expository Notes of Dr. Thomas Constable: Micah*, 1–4, https://planobiblechapel. org/tcon/notes/pdf/micah.pdf.

and do many miracles in Your name?' The I will announce to them, 'I never knew you! Depart from Me, you lawbreakers!'"

God saw the religious and the evil side of the people. J. Vernon McGee noted that God "cannot overlook dishonesty, violence, crookedness, lying, and deceit"[2] (vv. 9–12). Because of Judah's sin, God's judgment was coming (vv. 13–16). God's people had followed in the path of Omri and Ahab—two kings that were a father and a son—who experienced God's judgment.

Micah 7:1–4: Micah did not take pleasure in pronouncing judgment on his own people. He declared, "How sad for me!" (v. 1). This lament was common amongst prophets.

Jeremiah wrote, "If my head were a spring of water, my eyes a fountain of tears, I would weep day and night over the slain of my dear people" (Jeremiah 9:1).

Isaiah wrote, "Woe is me for I am ruined because I am a man of unclean lips and live among a people of unclean lips, and because my eyes have seen the King, the LORD of Hosts" (Isaiah 6:5).

No matter what nation we live in, we should not primarily be concerned with the state of our nation. Instead, we should be concerned with the state of the men and women of God within our nation.

Micah announced, "Godly people have vanished from the land" (v. 2). Instead, they all were eager to commit violence, accomplish evil, demand bribes, and plot together for evil purposes (vv. 2–3). God's judgment would come soon because of these things. Wiersbe notes, "People need to be alert at this point."[3]

Micah 7:5–7: Micah exhorted the people that they would not be able to trust close friends. Things would get so bad they couldn't even trust "the woman who lies in your arms." Families would be no better: "A man's enemies are the men of his own household" (v. 6). Jesus used this image in Matthew 10: "For I came to turn a man against his father, a daughter against her mother, a daughter-in-law against her mother-in-law; and a man's enemies will be the members of his household" (Matthew 10:35–36). Whereas Micah warned that things would get so bad that one's own family couldn't be trusted, Jesus warned that as we walk with Him we will experience the same thing.

No matter how bad things got around Micah, he resolved to "look to the LORD" and "wait for the God of my salvation" (v. 7). David expressed a similar attitude: "At daybreak, LORD, You hear my voice; at daybreak I plead my case to You and watch expectantly" (Psalm 5:3). Micah was bothered by what he saw in his culture and among God's people. All Micah could do was to make

[2] J. Vernon McGee, "Outline for Micah," https://www.blueletterbible.org/Comm/mcgee_j_vernon/notes-outlines/micah/micah-outline.cfm.

[3] Warren W. Wiersbe, *The Wiersbe Bible Commentary: Old Testament* (Colorado Springs: David C. Cook, 2007), 400.

sure that his own focus was on the Lord. MacArthur states, "In spite of his dire circumstances, Micah, as a watchman, would intently look for evidence of God working, trusting God to act in His own time and way."[4]

Micah 7:8–13: Beginning in verse 8, Israel spoke. In verses 8–10, Israel began to confess and repent of its sin. Legal language was picked up again, as Israel admitted that God would bring justice to them, after He brought His case against them (v. 9). A day would come when the remnant of God's people would return to Israel (vv. 10–13).

Micah 7:14–20: The Lord promised that He would gather the remnant of His people. He promised He would "perform miracles for them as in the days of your exodus from the land of Egypt" (v. 15). The enemies of His people would "tremble in the presence of Yahweh our God; they will stand in awe of You" (v. 17).

In spite of God's people turning away from Him, He promised to pass over all of their sin and delight in the remnant that remained faithful. His promises remained unconditional. Israel's sins would not stop God from fulfilling the promises He made to Abraham (v. 20). Psalm 89:33 says, "But I will not withdraw My faithful love from him or betray My faithfulness." God's ultimate restoration of Israel, and the ultimate fulfillment of the covenant He made with Abraham, will come in the millennium.

Closing

There are 13 places in the major and minor prophets where God promised to restore Israel. The greatest revival of all time is coming to the people of Israel. God promised they would be restored to their land and to their ultimate *Shepherd*, Jesus.

The Daily Word

The prophet Micah continued to declare the Lord's message, *patterned with both warning and hope to God's people*, the nation of Israel. He pointed out how they outwardly performed all the offerings and sacrifices, trying to please God. Yet God continued to desire their heart offerings. Micah explained what the Lord required of His people—*to act justly, to love faithfulness, and to walk humbly with Him*. However, God's people continued to turn against Him. Therefore, the Lord judged them and brought punishment. As the pattern went, Micah concluded

---

[4] "Micah 7 Commentary," Precept Austin, March 31, 2023, https://www.preceptaustin.org/micah_7_commentary.

with a message of hope for God's people, reminding them of His character and His promises.

Today, remember the Lord your God is able to remove your sin and forgive your rebellion. He does not hold on to His anger forever because He delights in faithful love. He will have compassion on you again and again. He promises to cast your sin into the depths of the sea. He promises to show you loyalty and be faithful to His covenant promise. As you seek the Lord daily, He asks you *to act justly, to love faithfulness, and to walk humbly with Him as your God*. He desires the sacrifice and devotion of your heart.

Mankind, He has told you what is good
and what it is the Lord requires of you:
to act justly,
to love faithfulness,
and to walk humbly with your God. —Micah 6:8

Further Scripture: Psalm 89:33–34; Micah 7:7, 18–20

Questions

1. According to Micah 6:8, what does the Lord require of you?

2. As God pled with Israel to repent in Micah 6:1–7, what things did He remind them of?

3. Micah could not find an upright man in the land (Micah 7: 1–4). How does this compare to today? Who should we not put our trust in? Who should we look to?

4. What did the Holy Spirit highlight to you in Micah 6—7 through the reading or the teaching?

Lesson 14: Nahum 1—3

Burden Bearer: The Burden Bearer

Teaching Notes

Intro

If you're like me, you haven't really studied the book of Nahum before. The book is named after the prophet Nahum who took a warning to Nineveh. The prophet Jonah didn't want to go to Nineveh so he actually ran away. However, when Jonah finally obeyed and delivered God's message, the people repented and turned back to God. Nahum brought a message years later that God's destruction was coming and could not be aborted. The name Nahum means "'comfort' or 'consolation'" and was a shortened form of Nehemiah.[1] Nahum 1:15 gives a picture of what was to come: "The wicked one will never again march through you; he will be entirely wiped out."

Nahum was an Elkoshite, either by birth or in ministry. MacArthur states that the exact location of Elkosh is unknown, but could "include Al Qosh, situated in the northern Iraq (thus Nahum would have been a descendant of the exiles taken to Assyria in 722 BC), Capernaum ('town of Nahum'), or a location in southern Judah."[2] The date of the book is not certain. Since Nineveh was described as a world power, Nahum must have written it before her fall in 612 BC, and probably before the death of Ashurbanipal in 626 BC, since the nation began losing power after his death. Since Nahum mentioned the fall of No Amon, or Thebes, it can probably be dated in "the mid-seventh century during the reign of Manasseh (c. 695–642 BC)."[3]

One hundred years after Nineveh repented, "She returned to idolatry, violence, and arrogance. She was at the height of her power" at the time.[4] God used the Babylonian army under King Nabopolassar and his son Nebuchadnezzar to bring about the fall of Assyria/Nineveh in 612 BC.[5]

---

[1] John MacArthur, *The MacArthur Bible Commentary* (Nashville: Thomas Nelson, 2005), 1022.

[2] MacArthur, 1022.

[3] MacArthur, 1022.

[4] MacArthur, 1022.

[5] MacArthur, 1022.

The book of Nahum is actually a sequel to the book of Jonah. There's a lesson for evangelists in this. The people truly repented under Jonah, but later generations did not. We can lead people to the Lord, but we cannot make them have a true walk with the Lord.

MacArthur explains that "Nineveh was proud of her reputed invulnerable city, her walls reaching 100 feet high and with a moat 150 feet wide and 60 feet deep."[6] However, Nahum 1:8 states that Nineveh would be destroyed with an overwhelming flood, and according to Nahum 3:11, the city would be lost from sight. "After its destruction in 612 BC, the site was not rediscovered until 1842 AD."[7]

Teaching

Nahum 1:2–6: Nahum described God as jealous, avenging, and fierce in His wrath. Through God's power, the clouds are just dust beneath His feet. He can rebuke the sea and it will dry up and He can make all rivers run dry. Even the great cedars (flowers) of Lebanon wither, the mountains quake, and the hills melt before Him (vv. 2–6).

Nahum 1:7–13: Our phrase for how Jesus is seen in the book of Nahum is *Burden Bearer*, and it is found in verse 7—"He cares for those who take refuge in Him" (Psalm 46:1; Isaiah 33:2–4; 37:3–7, 29–38). God would destroy Nineveh and it would not rise again (vv. 8–10). The "wicked counselor" in verse 11 "suggests satanic influence on the leadership, identified as the king of Assyria," possibly Sennacherib "who invaded Judah in 701 BC and of whom Isaiah speaks in similar language (Isaiah 10:7)."[8] Despite their great power and huge armies, Assyria would no longer threaten or imprison Judah (vv. 12–13). Jesus displayed this same picture of taking on the burdens of the people (Isaiah 61; Matthew 11:28–30; Luke 4:18; 2 Corinthians 5:21). Christ took on the sin burden that was meant for us, and He carries it.

Nahum 1:14–15: Nahum described God's coming judgment. First, there would be no one left to carry on the name of the king or his people. Second, the carved idols and images of the Assyrian gods would be destroyed. And third, the king would be put to death (v. 14). However, there was One to come who would bring good news and proclaim peace (v. 15).

This was a good news/bad news prophecy. The bad news was that the Assyrians would be wiped off the face of the earth. The good news was that Judah

---

[6] MacArthur, 1023–24.

[7] MacArthur, 1023.

[8] MacArthur, 1024.

would be freed from the chains of the Assyrians and given peace. The crazy thing about all of this is that it would be the Babylonians who put it in motion and set God's people free from Assyria. Sadly, God's people would then face captivity again through the Babylonians.

Nahum 2:1–13: God explained that He was justified in the destruction of Nineveh because they had committed so many crimes.

Nahum 3:1–19: God explained the internal condition of the city and the external condition of the city. They were making and selling slaves, fighting and killing people without end, and engaging in prostitution, sorcery, and witchcraft. What happened in the downfall of Thebes would happen to Assyria. There would be no remedy for them. McGee compares the messages of Jonah and Nahum this way. The message of Jonah was "God will save today," and the message of Nahum was "God will destroy tomorrow."[9] McGee concludes, "God does not change; men do."[10]

Closing

God told the people to celebrate their festivals and to fulfill their covenant vows. In other words, He told them to walk out their relationship with Him. They were to proclaim the peace that could only come through the Lord, and they were to wait for the One who would bring the good news. There's evidence for this in the New Testament as well:

Matthew 28:18–20: "Then Jesus came near and said to them, 'All authority has been given to Me in heaven and on earth. Go, therefore, and make disciples of all nations, baptizing them in the name of the Father and of the Son and of the Holy Spirit, teaching them to observe everything I have commanded you. And remember, I am with you always, to the end of the age.'"

Romans 10:15: "And how can they preach unless they are sent? As it is written: How beautiful are the feet of those who announce the gospel of good things!"

Ephesians 2:17: "When the Messiah came, He proclaimed the good news of peace to you who were far away and peace to those who were near."

Ephesians 6:15: "And your feet sandaled with readiness for the gospel of peace."

Because of what Jesus did on the cross, He is our *Burden Bearer* and we have peace.

---

[9] J. Vernon McGee, "Outline of Nahum," https://www.blueletterbible.org/Comm/mcgee_j_vernon/notes-outlines/nahum/nahum-outline.cfm.

[10] McGee.

The Daily Word

The prophet Nahum brought a message of comfort to the Israelites and prophesied about the Lord's judgment on Nineveh and Assyria. He proclaimed that *the Lord is good, a stronghold in the day of distress. The Lord cares for those who take refuge in Him.* But Nahum also confirmed God would completely destroy Assyria for their destructive ways. Israel would no longer be in bondage to Assyria because the Lord would break off the yoke and tear off the shackles. The Lord would set them free, and one day, *the feet of One bringing good news and proclaiming peace would come.*

No matter what destructiveness is in your life, the Lord is your refuge and stronghold in your day of distress. Look to Jesus to be your burden bearer. *Whatever* you face today. *Whatever* feels heavy on your list, remember to seek the Lord with it. He will lighten your burdens. He will set you free. He will bring you peace. You are no longer in chains. You have been set free and made perfect through Jesus Christ. The Lord will bring justice to the destruction. *Now go* and walk in freedom and share the peace with those around you.

**The Lord is good,
a stronghold in a day of distress;
He cares for those who take refuge in Him.
But He will completely destroy Nineveh
with an overwhelming flood,
and He will chase His enemies into darkness. —Nahum 1:7–8**

Further Scripture: Nahum 1:13, 15; Matthew 11:30

Questions

1. To whom was the book of Nahum written, and what does it have in common with the book of Jonah?

2. Unlike the prophet Jonah who preached in the streets of Nineveh about 100 years earlier, what was the prophet Nahum sent to do?

3. What does Nahum 2:8 compare Nineveh to? What made Nineveh turn back to their old ways?

4. What does Nahum 3 say of the fate of Nineveh? How do some of the evil things Nineveh was doing compare to some of the evil that goes on in the world today? Should we fear God's wrath?

5. What did the Holy Spirit highlight to you in Nahum 1—3 through the reading or the teaching?

Lesson 15: Habakkuk 1—3

Coming Salvation: Habakkuk's Prophecy

Teaching Notes

Intro

This week, we not only finish up our study of the Minor Prophets, but we finish up the Old Testament books as well. The study of the Old Testament has been life-changing. So far in the Minor Prophets, we've studied Hosea, Joel, Amos, Obadiah, Jonah, Micah, and Nahum. The eighth Minor Prophet is Habakkuk.

The book of Habakkuk is named for its author, and the name means "one who embraces." MacArthur states, "By the end of the prophecy, this name becomes appropriate as the prophet clings to God regardless of his confusion about God's plans for His people."[1] Nothing is known about the prophet except what's provided within the book. Because even that information was given sparingly, some scholars suggest Habakkuk didn't need more information because he was already known at the time. Habakkuk was also a contemporary of (lived at the same time as) Jeremiah, Ezekiel, Daniel, and Zephaniah, and his message was for the southern kingdom of Judah. Habakkuk 1:6 mentions the Chaldeans (Babylonians), which suggests dating it to the late seventh century BC. MacArthur explains this would have been "shortly before Nebuchadnezzar began his military march through Nineveh (612 BC)"[2] and "Habakkuk's bitter lament (Habakkuk 1:2–4) may reflect a time period shortly after the death of Josiah (609 BC), days in which the godly king's reforms (2 Kings 23) were quickly overturned by his successor, Jehoiakim (Jeremiah 22:13–19)."[3] Habakkuk therefore covered this shift in world power from the Assyrians to the Babylonians.

Habakkuk prophesied during the end of the Assyrian Empire and the beginning of the Babylonian Empire. These and other world powers will all fall before God's kingdom. The Babylonian empire under King Nabopolassar and then his son Nebuchadnezzar attacked the Assyrians, overthrowing their capital city of Nineveh in 612 BC and finally defeating them in Carchemish in 605 BC. While

---

[1] John MacArthur, *The MacArthur Bible Commentary* (Nashville: Thomas Nelson, 2005), 1028.

[2] MacArthur, 1028.

[3] MacArthur, 1028.

Necho the Egyptian king traveled through Judah to assist Assyria, he came against King Josiah and the king's army. In the battle, King Josiah was killed. King Josiah had led reforms in Judah that found the mission book of the Law in the temple. Through the Law, Josiah led the people to renew their covenant with the Lord in 622 BC. However, under the leadership of his sons, Judah moved away from the Lord and back to its worship of idols and pagan gods.[4]

Our phrase for Habakkuk for where we can see Jesus is *Coming Salvation*. This can be seen in Habakkuk 2:3 and 3:18. (Hebrews 10:37.)

- *Habakkuk 2:3*: "For the vision is yet for the appointed time; it testifies about the end and will not lie. Though it delays, wait for it, since it will certainly come and not be late."
- *Habakkuk 3:18*: "Yet, I will triumph in Yahweh; I will rejoice in the God of my salvation!"

Teaching

Habakkuk 1:1–17: Habakkuk explained that he had seen God's vision of what was to come (v. 1a) and questioned why God wasn't listening to his prayers (vv. 1b–4). God responded that Habakkuk should be utterly astounded at what was happening in the world (vv. 5–8). God was raising up the Babylonians to take over His own people through violence (vv. 9–11). Habakkuk then questioned God again (vv. 12–17). Habakkuk said the Babylonians were so wicked that they would draw the Judeans into their net as well.

Habakkuk 2:1–5: Habakkuk said he would stand at his post until he heard from God (v. 1). God replied in verses 2–5 and told Habakkuk to write His response so everyone could see it. MacArthur noted, "Habakkuk was to record the vision to preserve it for posterity, so that all who read it would know of the certainty of its fulfillment."[5] This was so the vision would testify about the end times (v. 3a). It would happen in God's timing (v. 3b). In verse 4, God described Babylon as having an inflated ego with no integrity, who would be conquered by the righteous one (Romans 1:17; Galatians 3:11; Hebrews 10:37–38). We are to live like the righteous one without drawing back from the world. On the other hand, the arrogant man is never satisfied and always wants more for himself (v. 5).

Habakkuk 2:6–20: In verse 6 God began to outline the five woes that the arrogant would face:

---

[4] MacArthur, 1028.

[5] MacArthur, 1031.

- First, *woe to the arrogant who would amass great wealth* that would not belong to him permanently. This continued the picture of Babylon's aggressiveness against other nations, even taking things that belonged to others. Verse 7 describes these as Babylon's "creditors" who would one day collect against them (v. 7). Babylon would fall to all the nations that they had captured (v. 8).
- Second, *woe to the dishonest man who thinks wealth would save him* (v. 9). His dishonesty will be shouted out by the stones in the wall and the rafters in the ceiling (vv. 10–11).
- Third, *woe to the one who builds a city through bloodshed*, for their efforts would come to nothing (vv. 12–14). Only the millennial kingdom will bring back God's glory into the world.
- Fourth, *woe to him who makes his neighbors drunk* so he could take advantage against them (vv. 15–17).
- Fifth, *woe to him who crafted idols from wood or iron* that could not speak or have any power (vv. 18–19).

Verse 20 concludes, "But the Lord is in His holy temple; let everyone on earth be silent in His presence." MacArthur explains the use of "silence" here: "In contrast to the silence of the idols, the living, sovereign ruler of the universe calls all the earth to be silent before Him. None can assert his independence from Him; all the earth must worship in humble submission (Psalm 46:20; Isaiah 53:15)."[6]

Habakkuk 3:2–16: In chapter 3, Habakkuk offered another prayer. He asked God to revive His work in this time (v. 2). Habakkuk described God's splendor covering the heavens and the earth as full of His praise. Even the mountains shudder before the Lord, and the sun and moon stand still in His presence (vv. 3–15). Habakkuk responded in praise and his willingness to "quietly wait for the day of distress to come against" those who invaded them (v. 16).

Closing

That creates a serious question for all of us. In this time of waiting on the Lord, do we wait patiently? Or do we complain while we wait upon the Lord? Do you believe that God is coming? Habakkuk believed God was going to show up, even though the Babylonians were already on their way. Habakkuk concluded with this statement of trust with these words (Habakkuk 3:19): "Yahweh, my Lord is my strength; He makes my feet like those of a deer and enables me to walk on mountain heights!"

---

[6] MacArthur, 1031.

The Daily Word

The prophet Habakkuk lamented to the Lord about the injustice and violence in the world. As He faced the dilemma of understanding God's ways, he asked:

How long, LORD, must I call for help
and You do not listen
or cry out to You about violence
and You do not save?

. . . .

Why do You tolerate wrongdoing? (Habakkuk 1:2–3)

After God answered, *Habakkuk displayed faith* in the midst of not understanding. He demonstrated trust in the midst of trials. He found hope in the Lord in the midst of despair. How? By faith, *Habakkuk believed in the God of his salvation.*

What do you do when God isn't showing up the way you asked Him to? What do you do when you don't understand the injustice around you? Yes, you have questions for God. But right now, today, pause for just a minute. By faith, choose to declare: "*Yet* I will triumph in Yahweh; I will rejoice in the God of my salvation! Yahweh my Lord is my strength; He makes my feet like those of a deer and enables me to walk on mountain heights!" Fix your eyes on Jesus, rather than on the problem. As you turn to the Lord, give Him thanks. Choose to trust, even in the midst of not understanding. Rejoice *always*.

Yet I will triumph in Yahweh;
I will rejoice in the God of my salvation!
Yahweh my Lord is my strength;
He makes my feet like those of a deer
and enables me to walk on mountain heights! —Habakkuk 3:18–19

Further Scripture: Habakkuk 1:2–3; Philippians 4:6–7; Hebrews 4:16

Questions

1. Habakkuk 1:3 asks, "Why do You make me see iniquity, and cause me to look on wickedness?" Do you ever feel like this toward God? Do you ever wonder why He is not doing anything to stop sin and wickedness in the world?

2. Habakkuk 1:5 says, "Look among the nations! Observe! Be astonished! Wonder! Because I am doing something in your days. You would not believe if you were told." Who was talking here, and what do you think He was referring to?

3. God told Habakkuk that He was raising up the Chaldeans to bring judgment upon the Jews. Name some other places in Scripture where God used wicked people to discipline His own people (Judges 3:1–4; Jeremiah 21:12). Do you think He still does this today? If so, name some situations or times in history when this has happened.

4. What have we made with our own hands that could be considered idols today? What idols do you need to lay down and quit depending on to make you happy in your own life? (Habakkuk 2:18)

5. Habakkuk 3:3 states, "God comes from Teman, and the Holy One from Mount Paran. His glory covered the heavens, and the earth was full of His praise." What do you think Teman and Mount Paran meant or were referring to, since God doesn't come from anything and He made everything?

6. Habakkuk 3:13 states, "You went forth for the salvation of Your people, for the salvation of Your anointed. You struck the head of the house of evil to lay him open from thigh to neck. Selah." How does this verse point to Jesus?

7. What did the Holy Spirit highlight to you in Habakkuk 1—3 through the reading or the teaching?

Lesson 16: Zephaniah 1—3

Mighty Warrior: The Day of the Lord

Teaching Notes

Intro

We are starting a new book today! It's not very big. In fact, some people have a hard time finding it. These small books are called Minor Prophets because they are so short. Size is really the only difference between the Major and Minor Prophets. It's is important to remember that during the time of Zephaniah, the kingdom was split. Zephaniah served and prophesied in the Southern Kingdom.

With each of the 12 minor prophets, the book of prophecy bears the name of the its author. Little is known about Zephaniah. His name means, "the Lord hides." MacArthur states, "The prophet himself dates his message during the reign of Josiah (630–609 BC). The moral and spiritual conditions detailed in the book (Zephaniah 1:4–6; 3:1–7) seem to place the prophecy prior to Josiah's reform, when Judah was still functioning in idolatry and wickedness."[1] In 2 Chronicles, Josiah tore down the alters, burned the bones of false prophets, and broke the carved idols (around 628 BC). Wiersbe points out this led many to believe that Zephaniah prophesied from 635–625 BC, around the same time as Jeremiah.[2] The dates are important because we know that during this point in time the Israelites had no hope.

During this time politically, the world power had gone from the Assyrians to the Babylonians. According to MacArthur, Judah benefited from the changing politics in the region as Assyria began to lose power and Babylon began to grow stronger. In fact, Babylon's impending threat over Assyria actually caused Assyria to loosen its grip on Judah, "bringing an element of independence to Judah for the first time in 50 years. Spiritually, the reigns of Hezekiah's son Manasseh, extended over four decades, and his grandson Amon, lasting only two [years], were marked by wickedness and apostasy (2 Kings 21; 2 Chronicles 33)."[3] Before

---

[1] John MacArthur, *The MacArthur Bible Commentary* (Nashville: Thomas Nelson, 2005), 1036.

[2] Warren W. Wiersbe, *The Bible Exposition Commentary: Isaiah–Malachi* (Colorado Spring: David C. Cook, 2002), 425.

[3] MacArthur, 1036.

Josiah's reform, the land was characterized by wickedness. After the discovery of the book of the Law, Josiah started reform and led the people to once again worship and seek the Lord.

Zephaniah's message came during a time of evil and hopelessness, before Josiah's reform. The message of Zephaniah really focused on the Day of the Lord. The final days for the Israelites were near. Their judgment was coming at the hands of King Nebuchadnezzar of Babylon (605–586 BC). MacArthur explains that Zephaniah's message "looks beyond to the far fulfillment in the judgment of Daniel's seventieth week (Zephaniah 1:18; 3:8)."[4] The message was, yes, dark times are coming, but seek the Lord during these times. Our phrase for where Jesus is seen in Zephaniah is *Mighty Warrior*.

Teaching

Zephaniah 1:1–6: Zephaniah traced his genealogy back through four generations, all the way back to King Hezekiah. He was the only prophet to come from royal blood (v. 1). Zephaniah wrote there would be judgment on the entire earth. The world would be swept away (vv. 2–3,) a clear comparison to the Genesis flood (Genesis 6:9; 7:23). Remember, God promised worldwide destruction would not happen again until the end of days. God will continue to remove earthly living things until He will judge all of humankind. Starting in verse four, Zephaniah spelled out the judgment on Judah. Wiersbe states Zephaniah "relates the Day of the Lord to both the Jews and the Gentiles."[5]

Zephaniah 1:7: In verse 7, Zephaniah talked about Judah becoming God's sacrifice. God's judgment was the sacrifice of Judah, and the guest who was coming to deliver God's judgment was the Babylonian army. The Day of the Lord refers to the time after the seven years of tribulation, spelled out by John in Revelation. The Israelites didn't have the picture of the Day of Lord like we do today.

Zephaniah 1:8–10: The statement, "all who are dressed in foreign clothing," referred to those who had been focusing on the wrong gods and the wrong things. They had dressed in fakeness, pretending in ways in which they should not have been living.

Zephaniah 1:11: Wiersbe states, "Zephaniah must have been a resident of Jerusalem, for he knew the layout of the city."[6] He went into really specific details about the city. On Zephaniah's mention of merchants, MacArthur wrote, "Merchants

---

[4] MacArthur, 1036–37.

[5] Wiersbe, 42.

[6] Wiersbe, 427.

made wealthy from dishonest gain were singled out to depict the anguish of the coming judgment."[7]

Zephaniah 1:12: This is a very interesting posture. If you were going to apply the description of "men who settled down" to today, it would be a complacent believer.

Zephaniah 1:14–18: Zephaniah described the Day of the Lord for Judah, but also, the great tribulation at the end of the seven years. The Day of the Lord was coming for the Israelites, but it is also coming for us. McGee describes the Day of the Lord as "A day of fear."[8] I don't want us to miss that this seems like a great time to hide. No matter where you are, you are not going to be able to escape or hide. Not just Judah, but everyone would experience a horrifying end.

Zephaniah 2: Zephaniah urged the Israelites to pray for deliverance. He also encouraged them to seek the Lord, to seek righteousness, and to seek humility. Maybe the Lord will hide you. We are all in need of the Lord's protection from the Day of the Lord. It will be hell on earth. Zephaniah shifted from judgment on Judah to the entire nation. Then judgment would come on Ethiopia, and then Assyria. The people of Judah had become comfortable, believing God would do neither good nor bad. When we see that posture of complacence, then we will see God bring about destruction. We must not be complacent. We need to be ready for the return of Jesus at any given time.

Zephaniah 3: Zephaniah discussed the coming judgment that Jerusalem deserved. You could see so many cities in the world deserving similar judgment. Again, we see the Armageddon mentality. McGee writes, "This is Armageddon, which ends with the return of Christ to the earth."[9] God's love is so strong for His people, His jealousy is so strong for His people, and His anger so strong against the other nations that He goes before them in battle.

Closing

The battle of Armageddon is when God will wipe out all the other nations. The phrase in Zephaniah is the *Mighty Warrior*, which points to Jesus. Jesus is the one coming back to save His people. He's going to fight for us, and He is also going to love us.

---

[7] MacArthur, 1038.

[8] J. Vernon McGee, "Notes for Zephaniah," https://www.blueletterbible.org/Comm/mcgee_j_vernon/notes-outlines/zephaniah/zephaniah-outline.cfm.

[9] McGee.

The Daily Word

The prophet Zephaniah proclaimed that judgment would come for Jerusalem, for Judah, for all the nation, and even for the whole earth. Zephaniah proclaimed the Day of the Lord for his current time, but ultimately, for the end. And yet *Zephaniah also declared that God would gather a remnant* in His amazing grace, offsetting His jealous anger against those seeking evil. God is a warrior. He is mighty to save. The Lord will rejoice over His people with gladness and delight in them with shouts of joy. He is in their midst and will save.

Oh, friend, the Lord will bring you quietness in the midst of destruction and despair. Imagine the picture of a battle . . . As you look out over the horizon, you see a warrior standing out among the others, victoriously riding toward you. As you watch this warrior, you know he is coming to rescue you. As he arrives to you, he celebrates with a cheer of joy. He cares for your safety and saves you. This is a picture of the love of your heavenly Father. Look up from the battle. Look up and seek the Lord alone. He is in your midst. He fights for you and will rescue you. He delights over you with shouts of joy. He rejoices over you with gladness. Do not fear. The Lord is near.

On that day it will be said to Jerusalem:
"Do not fear;
Zion, do not let your hands grow weak.
Yahweh your God is among you,
a warrior who saves.
He will rejoice over you with gladness.
He will bring you quietness with His love.
He will delight in you with shouts of joy." —Zephaniah 3:16–17

Further Scripture: Deuteronomy 7:21; Psalm 9:10; Zephaniah 2:3

Questions

1. Why do you think Zephaniah traced his lineage in such specific detail in Zephaniah 1:1?

2. Was Zephaniah referring to the past or the future in Zephaniah 1:14–18?

3. What do you think the "Fish Gate" and "Second Quarter," from Zephaniah 1:10 were?

4. According to Zephaniah and other Old Testament prophets, how does God discipline His own people differently from those who bring anything against them? How is this like the way we discipline our own children when compared to how we feel when someone else tries to discipline, hurt, or attack them?

5. Why do you think the people of Israel would not receive instruction from the Lord after hearing the warnings from the prophets (Zephaniah 3:7)? How are we like them today?

6. What did the Holy Spirit highlight to you in Zephaniah 1—3 through the reading or the teachings?

Lesson 17: Haggai 1—2

Greater Temple: The Temple of the Lord

Teaching Notes

Intro

We are in the ninth segment of our study through the Bible! We finish up with the book of Revelation next. We have gone through nine Minor Prophets thus far. I am willing to bet that most of us have not really studied the book of Haggai that often. Hebrews 12:26 is the only place in the New Testament that Haggai is quoted. Little is known about the writer of Haggai. He is mentioned in Ezra 5:1 and 6:14, and both also mention Zechariah. There is no record of Haggai's occupation, and he is the only person mentioned in the Old Testament with his name.[1] MacArthur states, "Haggai 2:3 may suggest that he had seen the glory of Solomon's temple before it was destroyed, making him at least 70 years of age when writing this prophecy."[2] Our phrase for Jesus in Haggai is the *Greater Temple*.

Haggai's prophecies happened in a four-month time frame in the second year of Darius, the king of Persia (521–486 BC). It is likely Haggai returned to Jerusalem from Babylon 18 years earlier with Zerubbabel. After captivity, Israel was allowed to return home under the civil leadership of Zerubbabel and the spiritual leadership of Joshua, the high priest, in 538 BC. MacArthur explains, "In 536 BC, they began to rebuild the temple, but opposition from neighbors and indifference by the Jews caused the work to be abandoned. Sixteen years later Haggai and Zechariah were commissioned by the Lord to stir up the people to (1) rebuild the temple, but also to (2) restore their spiritual priorities."[3]

The theme in Haggai is, "Let's rebuild the temple." In fact, Haggai was like a spiritual contractor. God motivated them by bringing a drought causing crop failure because of their failed spiritual priorities. The temple has always represented the Lord's presence. However, when the temple was destroyed, the people believed God's glory had left. The rebuilding of the temple was essentially

---

[1] John MacArthur, *The MacArthur Bible Commentary* (Nashville: Thomas Nelson, 2005), 1042.

[2] MacArthur, 1042.

[3] MacArthur, 1042.

welcoming the presence of God back into their lives. The rebuilding of the temple pointed to the *Greater Temple*. I want to look at the progression of the temple to help us understand Haggai's writings better.

MacArthur outlines the details of the temples of the Bible:

1. The Tabernacle was the first temple in Scripture and dated around 1444 BC (Exodus 25:30, Leviticus 10:1–7).

2. Solomon's temple was built by King Solomon, David's son (966–586 BC). David wanted to build a temple to God, but God chose Solomon to do it (2 Samuel 7:1–29).

3. Zerubbabel's temple was prophesized by both Haggai and Zechariah and was built between 516–169 BC (Ezra 3:1–8).

4. Herod's temple was a restoration and renewal project of Zerubbabel's temple (19 BC–AD 70). It was destroyed by Rome (Mark 13:2; John 2:20).

5. The present temple is now the body of believers who are, temporarily, the temple of God. That will change with the return of the Messiah (1 Corinthians 6:19–20).

6. The temple of Revelation 11 is where the antichrist will stand during the Great Tribulation (Daniel 9:27; Matthew 24:15).

7. Ezekiel's millennial temple will be built in the millennium. It was described in the book of Ezekiel and will be built by the Messiah (Ezekiel 40:1—42:20).

8. Eternal temple of His presence will be the greatest temple ever built and will be a spiritual temple (Revelation 21:22).[4]

Why unpack of all this? Because really, Haggai was pointing to Zerubbabel's temple, and he was also beginning to unpack the Ezekiel and/or the eternal temple.

Teaching

Haggai 1:1–11: J. Vernon McGee explains verses 1–11 were "a challenge to the people."[5] The people were content to live in their houses with their material wealth while the temple lay in ruin. Possibly the word of the Lord came to Haggai to deliver during a holy feast. The Lord said the people put off rebuilding His temple. Instead they chose to live comfortably in their paneled houses while His house was in ruins (vv. 1–4). Haggai explained the Israelites were never satisfied and always wanted more. God told them to go to the mountains, bring back wood, and rebuild His house so He would be glorified. God explained that

---

[4] MacArthur, 1047.

[5] J. Vernon McGee, "Outline of Haggai," https://www.blueletterbible.org/Comm/mcgee_j_vernon /notes-outlines/haggai/haggai-outline.cfm.

because His house had not been rebuilt, He had brought destruction to their crops (v. 9). God withheld the dew from them, creating drought that killed the crops (vv. 10–11).

Haggai 1:12–15: Something in Haggai's words convicted the people that they needed to obey God's command. King Zerubbabel, the high priest Joshua, and the entire remnant of the people obeyed (v. 12). Haggai reminded the people that God was with them (v.13)! The Lord stirred up the spirits of Zerubbabel, Joshua, and all the people (v. 14). I think that means they became passionate about rebuilding the house of the Lord. They began the work on the new temple "on the twenty-fourth day of the sixth month, in the second year of King Darius" (v. 15).

Haggai 2:1–9: One month later, the people were getting discouraged with the task of rebuilding. God sent Haggai with another message—be strong and obedient (vv. 1–4). Once again God reminded the people that His Spirit was with them (v. 5). The Lord of Hosts promised He would again shake the heavens, the earth, and the sea, and every nation on earth, and they would bring glory to His house (vv. 6–7). This is a picture of the millennial kingdom. God described the new temple as "greater than the first," meaning it would be greater than Zerubbabel's temple (vv. 8–9). This was a foreshadowing of the *Greater Temple* in Revelation 21:22.

Haggai 2:10–19: Seven months later (the ninth month), God gave Haggai His message to deliver again. First, God says to Haggai, question whether or not something that had been set apart for Him that had touched something unconsecrated would become holy. The answer was no. Second question, God had him ask whether or not something that had been touched by someone who was defiled by contact with corpse would also be defiled. The answer was yes. The holiness did not transfer, but the unholiness did. Haggai explained that the people's work and all they offered was defiled because they were unholy. However, because they had obeyed God and laid the foundation of the temple on that very day, God promised to bless them. Although they had no seed in the granary and nothing growing on the trees, God would bless them with prosperity.

Haggai 2:20–23: God promised He would overturn royal thrones and destroy the power of the Gentile kingdoms. He would give divine leadership to the nation through Zerubbabel.

Closing

The most exciting thing about Haggai goes back to the list of temples. The people didn't want to build the temple. They wanted to stay in the good old days of comfort they had gotten used to. But, God had something better and greater for them when they let go of themselves. What we will ultimately see in the end is all these things come to be when Jesus returns (Revelation 21:22).

The Daily Word

The prophet Haggai spoke to the people after the Babylonian captivity regarding their lifestyle. He commanded them to rebuild the temple after its destruction. The prophet confirmed the word of the Lord saying, *I am with you*. He longed for them to *consider carefully* how they lived. Their choice to live faithfully and obediently mattered to the Lord. They had misplaced their priorities upon returning to Jerusalem. God had a *greater temple* for them, but they had to turn to God and *carefully consider* their ways.

Just as Haggai spoke to the Israelites, the same is true for you. The Lord longs to bless you and restore you. Therefore, consider your actions. Consider your ways. In this volatile world full of temptations, with the enemy luring and deceiving you, you must *consider carefully* how you live. *Pray*. Seek the Lord. Ask for clarity and confirmation. Walk humbly. Do not fear, for God is with you. He wants to rebuild His love in you. Jesus will provide you peace because He *is* peace. Today, *carefully consider* your decisions, actions, and words, and walk with the Lord. It matters to God. And He has something even greater for you.

Consider carefully from this day forward; from the twenty-fourth day of the ninth month, from the day the foundation of the Lord's temple was laid; consider it carefully. —Haggai 2:18

Further Scripture: Haggai 2:9, 15–17; Ephesians 5:15–17

Questions

1. Haggai the prophet received a message from the Lord to Zerubbabel, the governor of Judah, and Joshua, the high priest, in Haggai 1:1–2. What did Haggai tell them the people were saying? What were the people busy doing instead (Haggai 1:4, 9)?

2. How were the people building their own houses while God's house was neglected (Ezekiel 34:2; 1 Timothy 1:3–4)? (A situation that might be similar today is when some pastors build their own ministries but neglect the building of God's kingdom.)

3. What was the outcome of the people neglecting the rebuilding of God's house (Haggai 1:6, 10–11)? What outcome do you observe with churches today who are busy building their separate "kingdoms" rather than pursuing building the Church, which is the body of Christ? (Romans 12:5; 1 Corinthians 12:12–27; Ephesians 3:6; 5:23; Colossians 1:18)

4. How can we learn from the leadership and remnant of Judah in their response to the message from the Lord (Haggai 1:12)? Is this how you typically respond to the Lord's chastisement and discipline?

5. How would you feel and respond if the Lord's message in Haggai 2:4 were being spoken to you?

6. Do you believe the word from the Lord in Haggai 2:9 is a prophetic message about the coming of the Messiah and the new covenant? Why?

7. What did the Holy Spirit highlight to you in Haggai 1—2 through the reading or the teaching?

Lesson 18: Zechariah 1—4

Pierced One: Zechariah's Vision

Teaching Notes

Intro

Today we start our study in Zechariah. This is the fourth new book this week! Most scholars accept that the book is named after its author, the prophet Zechariah. The name Zechariah was used more than 29 times for people in the Old Testament, and it means "The Lord remembers." MacArthur explains Zechariah "is second only to Isaiah in the breadth of the prophets' writings about Messiah."[1] There is so much about the Messiah in Zechariah.

MacArthur points out that Zechariah was a priest just as Jeremiah and Ezekiel were: "According to tradition, he was a member of the Great Synagogue, a council of 120 originated by Nehemiah and presided over by Ezra. This council later developed into the ruling elders of the nation, called the Sanhedrin."[2] Zechariah was born in Babylon and returned to Jerusalem in the first group of exiles that included his grandfather. Some scholars suggest Zechariah's father, Berechiah, died at a young age and never followed in his father's place as a priest. The book of Zechariah is precisely dated in Zechariah 1:1 as 520 BC, the second year of Darius' rule. Zechariah was a prophet during the same time as Haggai but was probably younger than Haggai (Zechariah 2:4). No information is known about how long Zechariah served as a prophet. His last prophecy that was dated (Zechariah 7:4) was given approximately two years later than his first. Therefore both of his prophecies were given at the same time as Haggai's prophecies were given.

In 538 BC, under Cyrus the Persian's reign, 50,000 captives were allowed to return to Israel from Babylon. Once there, the returned exiles began the work of rebuilding the temple in Jerusalem. The temple was completed in 516 BC. MacArthur explains, "Zechariah and Haggai were commissioned by the Lord to stir up the people to rebuild the temple."[3]

---

[1] John MacArthur, *The MacArthur Bible Commentary* (Nashville: Thomas Nelson, 2005), 1049.

[2] MacArthur, 1049.

[3] MacArthur, 1049–50.

MacArthur compared the two prophets: "Haggai's primary purpose was to rebuild the temple; his preaching has a tone of rebuke for the people's indifference, sin, and lack of trust in God. He was used to start the revival, while Zechariah was used to keep them going strong with a more positive emphasis, calling the people to repentance and reassuring them regarding future blessings."[4]

Zechariah is the most apocalyptic book in the Old Testament and had a message for the returning exiles as well as for the future.

Teaching

Zechariah 1:1–6: The Lord came to the prophet Zechariah because He was extremely angry with Zechariah's ancestors (vv. 1–2). God called for the people to return to Him so He could return to them (v. 3). God told the people not to be like their ancestors who did not heed the prophets' warning to return to Him (v. 4). God asked where those ancestors were and where the prophets who had delivered the rejected messages were (v. 5). They had all died.

Zechariah 1:7–11: In verse 7, the language changes, and Zechariah began to describe eight visions he had in one night. Remember that visions happen while wide awake, while dreams happen while sleeping. Through visions, God showed Zechariah something that happened directly in front of him. These visions were supposed to bring comfort to the people. The first vision was of a man riding a red horse under the myrtle trees. Behind the man were red, sorrel, and white horses (vv. 7–8). MacArthur explains, "The colors may speak of the work of the riders: red speaking of bloodshed and judgment, white speaking of victory, and sorrel or a brownish color is possibly a combination of the others."[5] Zechariah asked about what he was seeing, and an angel said he would explain (v. 9). The man who had ridden the red horse said the horses had been sent by the Lord to patrol the earth (v. 10). MacArthur describes them as "a symbolic, military description of angelic movement patrolling and reconnoitering on a global scale. The purpose is to ascertain the state of the enemy and to respond to God's will in engaging that enemy triumphantly."[6] They reported to the Angel of the Lord (probably the pre-incarnate Christ) that the whole earth was calm and quiet (v. 11). Through this vision, God promised prosperity for Israel.

Zechariah 1:12–17: The Angel of the Lord asked God how long He would continue to withhold His mercy from Judah (v. 12). God replied with words of comfort to the angel (v. 13). This is an interaction between Jesus, the pre-incarnate

---

[4] MacArthur, 1050.

[5] MacArthur, 1053.

[6] MacArthur, 1053.

Christ, and God His Father (Romans 8:34; Hebrews 7:25). God explained He still loved Judah and Jerusalem and was extremely angry with the nations who went against them (vv. 14–15). Therefore God would bring prosperity back to Jerusalem and to His cities in Zion (vv. 16–17). Since myrtle trees were associated with the booths for the Festival of Booths, this vision pointed to God's continued blessing and protection on His people. In Isaiah 41 and 55, myrtle trees were also connected to the messianic blessing.[7]

Zechariah 1:18–20: The second vision was of four horns, which were "a symbol of power and pride."[8] Zechariah was told they were the horns that scattered all of Israel (vv. 18–19), probably referring to Babylon, Medo-Persia, Greece, and Rome. Then Zechariah was shown four craftsmen who had come to terrify the nations that had scattered Judah (vv. 20–21). In this, God promised to judge the nations who attacked Israel.

Zechariah 2: The third vision was of a man with a measuring line (vv. 1–3). This was to show God's plan to rebuild and reestablish Jerusalem and God would dwell there again (vv. 10–16).

Zechariah 3: The fourth vision was of the high priest and a branch (vv. 1–7). This shows a cleansing that God would use with the high priest and the people of Israel as God rescued them (v. 8). McGee explains, "Neither Joshua nor Israel were contenders with Satan while clothed in their own righteousness. They must be clothed with the righteousness of Christ. Even a new patch on the old garment will not avail."[9] "My servant, the Branch" is another reference to Jesus (v. 8), and verse 10 points to the coming age.

Zechariah 4: The fifth vision was of the gold lampstand and two olive trees to show that God would rebuild the temple through Zerubbabel (vv. 1–7).

Closing

All of this will be reestablished in God's plan. Zechariah 12:10 says: "Then I will pour out a spirit of grace and prayer on the house of David and the residents of Jerusalem, and they will look at Me whom they pierced." We'll unpack that as we move through the rest of the book of Zechariah.

---

[7] MacArthur, 1052.

[8] MacArthur, 1054.

[9] J. Vernon McGee, "Outline of Nahum," https://www.blueletterbible.org/Comm/mcgee_j_vernon /notes-outlines/nahum/nahum-outline.cfm.

The Daily Word

After Israel returned from exile, the word of the Lord came upon the prophet Zechariah through a series of dreams. He dreamt about Joshua, the high priest, standing before the people in filthy clothes, a symbol of Israel and their unclean sin. Then Joshua received clean clothes. *Zechariah declared this symbol of hope and restoration* for Israel if they walked in obedience to the Lord. He challenged the people to wholeheartedly seek the Lord as they rebuilt the temple.

Jesus was pierced for your iniquities, and His grace washes away your filthy sin and guilt. Whoever believes in Jesus as Savior and humbly repents will be forgiven. Then the Lord will freely give you robes of righteousness. Therefore, confidently come before the Lord with a humble heart and receive His grace and mercy. The clean robe is not just put on over your old, dirty robe. *Jesus completely removes the filthy robe of shame and guilt.* You are a child of the King, a royal heir, and you have access to God the Father. He calls you worthy. He loves you. Picture a white robe neatly wrapped around you and receive His gift today.

Then I said, "Let them put a clean turban on his head." So a clean turban was placed on his head, and they clothed him in garments while the Angel of the Lord was standing nearby. Then the Angel of the Lord charged Joshua: "This is what the Lord of Hosts says: If you walk in My ways and keep My instructions, you will both rule My house and take care of My courts; I will also grant you access among these who are standing here." —Zechariah 3:5–7

Further Scripture: Zechariah 3:3–4; Galatians 2:20; Revelation 19:8

Questions

1. What do you think the Lord means in Zechariah 2:5, "For I will be a wall of fire around Jerusalem, and I will be the glory in her midst"? (Revelation 21:23; 22:5)

2. Read Zechariah 2:8: "For he who touches you touches the apple of My eye." Many people believe the church has replaced the Jews as God's chosen people. Do you think what they believe is true?

3. In Zechariah 2:10–11, the Lord told His people He was coming and would dwell in their midst. Do you think this was a foretelling of the Messiah physically coming to His people? (Isaiah 7:14; 9:6; Matthew 1:23; John 1:1, 14)

4. As he was standing in front of an angel in Zechariah 3:3, Joshua, the high priest, was wearing filthy garments. Read Zechariah 3:4 and Isaiah 64:6. What do these filthy garments represent?

5. If Joshua, the high priest, and his friends were a symbol according to Zechariah 3:8, what were they a symbol of?

6. Who do you think the two anointed ones standing by the Lord in Zechariah 4:14 were? (Zechariah 4:2–3, 11–14; Revelation 11:1–4)

7. What did the Holy Spirit highlight to you in Zechariah 1—4 through the reading or the teaching?

Lesson 19: Zechariah 5—8

Pierced One: Receiving the Prophetic Word

Teaching Notes

Intro

In teaching the book of Zechariah, I want to expand in a little different direction. The point of reviveSCHOOL is to see how Jesus is revealed in each book, especially in the Old Testament. In Zechariah, we see Jesus throughout the entire book as the *Pierced One*.

Reread Zechariah 1:1–6. This explains that all of the prophets, both major and minor, pointed to God's coming judgment and the eternal hope for the future. We have already covered Zechariah's first *five visions*:

1. Zechariah saw a man riding a red horse under the myrtle trees, with red, sorrel, and white horses and four horsemen who patrolled the earth. They found peace throughout, which did not make God happy because their peace was created against His people (Zechariah 1:7–8).
2. Zechariah saw four horns and four horsemen (Zechariah 1:18–20).
3. Zechariah saw a man with a measuring line (Zechariah 2:1–3).
4. Zechariah saw the high priest and a branch (Zechariah 3:1–8).
5. Zechariah saw the gold lampstand (Zechariah 4:1–14).

Zechariah clearly points to the future hope. Zechariah 12:10 refers to Jesus as the *Pierced One*: "Then I will pour out a spirit of grace and prayer on the house of David and the residents of Jerusalem, and they will look at Me whom they pierced. They will mourn for Him as one mourns for an only child and weep bitterly for Him as one weeps for a firstborn."

Teaching

Zechariah 5:1–4: Zechariah's *sixth vision* was of a flying scroll. The scroll was 30 feet long and 15 feet wide and was floating in the air. Zechariah asked what it was. The scroll listed the names of those who had sinned and had sworn falsely on it and referred to the coming curse of God. The scroll would enter into their homes and destroy it completely.

Zechariah 5:5–11: Zechariah's *seventh vision* was of a measuring basket. Again, Zechariah asked what it was. The angel lifted the lead cover to reveal a woman sitting in the basket who represented wickedness—the iniquity of the people. The angel pushed the woman back into the basket and covered her back up. Then two women approached on the winds with stork-like wings who took the basket up between the earth and sky. They took the basket to be placed as a shrine on a pedestal. They were removing the iniquity from the land and taking it away.

Zechariah 6:1–8: Remember that these were visions while Zechariah was awake, not dreaming while he was asleep. Job 33:14–17 states, "For God speaks time and again, but a person may not notice it. In a dream, a vision in the night, when deep sleep falls on people as they slumber in their beds, He uncovers their ears at that time and terrifies them with warnings, in order to turn a person from his actions and suppress his pride."

There are many examples of dreams in Scripture: Joseph interpreted Pharaoh's dreams; Joseph of Nazareth was warned to flee to Egypt to keep Jesus safe; Daniel had dreams that he took before King Nebuchadnezzar. Zechariah was given in one night all eight of these visions.

The first vision in Zechariah 1 was of four chariots and horses, and the eighth and final vision was of the same thing. He saw four chariots coming between two mountains made of bronze. Each chariot had different colored horses—red with the first, black with the second, white with the third, and dappled horses with the fourth. These were four spirits of heaven going out into the world after having been presented before the Lord.

Closing

I want us to look at seven practical things you need to know as God begins to speak to you through visions, dreams, and prophetic words:

1. *Be open to receive the Word of the Lord* (Zechariah 1:7–8; 4:1). Zechariah was willing to hear what God had to say. He didn't go back to sleep.
    *   Be an open receiver.
2. *Be humble enough to ask questions about the Word of the Lord* (Zechariah 1:9). Zechariah didn't hesitate to ask about what he saw and what it meant.
    *   Be a humble asker.
3. *Be faithful to record the Word of the Lord* (Zechariah 1—6). Zechariah carefully wrote down everything with complete details.
    *   Be a faithful recorder.

4. *Be true to the Word* (Zechariah 5:1–4). Don't flower it up, water it down, or embellish it. Zechariah reported it accurately, despite how it would be accepted.
    *   Be a thankful deliverer.
5. *Be watchful for the Messiah of the Word* (Zechariah 6:9–14). Zechariah delivered a prophetic word about the coming Messiah and proclaimed what was to come.
    *   Be a watchful witness.
6. *Be aware of practical application of the Word* (Zechariah 5:17—7:1–6, 9–10). Prophetic words have a practical application. Be careful of those with prophetic words that are not practical.
    *   Be a practical prophet.
7. *Be a life speaker!* Speak life. That is where the hope of the Lord begins to prosper.
    *   Be one who speaks life.

The rest of the chapter speaks of God healing the land, restoring the fortunes, and children running in the streets again. As you walk this out, be open, humble, faithful, practical, truthful, and life speaking.

The Daily Word

Zechariah spoke as a prophet to God's chosen people in Israel upon their return from exile. The Lord gave Zechariah prophetic messages of judgment but also of blessing and hope, through dreams and visions. When the people fasted in exile, the Lord saw their hearts were like rock and questioned, "Did you really fast for Me?" The Lord asked the remnant to walk in obedience and to fast with *pure hearts leaning into the Lord*. He promised joy, gladness, and cheerful festivals in return.

Fasting encourages you to purify your heart, mind, and soul before the Lord. It often forces you to face a challenging situation by removing the extras in your life and truly focusing on the Lord for your strength, your sustenance, and your hope. Today, pray about fasting. Then obediently begin your fast, remembering to keep your motives for fasting pure. Don't fast to lose weight, be more productive with your time, or to make someone else happy. *Fast with a pure and obedient heart.* Love truth and peace, trusting the Lord to powerfully move in your midst.

The Lord of Hosts says this: The fast of the fourth month, the fast of the fifth, the fast of the seventh, and the fast of the tenth will become times of joy,

gladness, and cheerful festivals for the house of Judah. Therefore, love truth and peace. —Zechariah 8:19

Further Scripture: Exodus 34:28; Zechariah 7:4–6; Luke 4:2–4

Questions

1. What were the meanings of Zechariah's final three visions? (Zechariah 5:1—6:8)

2. If the crown was placed on the head of Joshua, then who is the reference to the Branch in Zechariah 6:12? (Isaiah 11:1; Zechariah 3:8; John 12:13–15; 1 Timothy 6:13–16)

3. What are some facts that were given about the Messiah in Zechariah 6:12–15?

4. In Zechariah 6:13, the Branch is promised to build the Lord's temple. Who ended up building the second earthly temple, and who is going to be building the millennial temple? (Isaiah 2:2–4; Haggai 2:6–9; Zechariah 4:9–10)

5. How is the city of Jerusalem characterized in Zechariah 8 (Zechariah 8:3, 8, 16)? When will Jerusalem be called these things? Why is the city characterized like that? (Isaiah 6:3; John 14:6)

6. What did the Holy Spirit highlight to you in Zechariah 5—8 through the reading or the teaching?

Lesson 20: Zechariah 9—12

Pierced One: Mourning for the Pierced One

Teaching Notes

Intro

Zechariah is one of the neglected books we should spend more time studying because these chapters contain so much of a message of the Messiah. Our phrase for Jesus in Zechariah is the *Pierced One*. When they look at Christ, they will realize they have pierced Him, and they will mourn (Zechariah 12:10). And they will realize the only way they can be set free from captivity is to look upon the One they pierced.

We'll cover Zechariah 9—12 today, but let's begin with a summary. Zechariah was a prophet who, along with Haggai, wanted Israel to rebuild the temple. In eight visions, God painted a picture for Zechariah that stressed the potential of Israel. Zechariah communicated that redemption was coming.

Teaching

Zechariah 9:1–8: This oracle, or judgment, was against Hadrach, Damascus, Hamath, Tyre, and Sidon (vv. 1–4). In verses 5–8, judgment was pronounced against the Philistine cities of Ashkelon, Gaza, Ekron, and Ashdod along the Mediterranean coast.

Zechariah 9:9–10: Verse 9 is one of the verses in the book that describes the Messiah. As J. Vernon McGee said, "It's the triumphal entry of Christ when He came into Jerusalem (Matthew 21:5)."[1] This verse describes Palm Sunday. John 12:15 says, "Fear no more, Daughter Zion. Look, your King is coming, sitting on a donkey's colt." When comparing Matthew 21 and John 12 with Zechariah 9:9, there's something missing. Both the gospel passages omit: "Rejoice greatly, Daughter Zion! Shout in triumph, Daughter Jerusalem!" This part will be fulfilled in Christ's second coming. Like other prophets, Zechariah includes a lot of "already, but not yet" prophecies. With Christ's second advent, peace will come

---

[1] Warren W. Wiersbe, *The Wiersbe Bible Commentary: Old Testament* (Colorado Springs: David C. Cook, 2007), 1519.

to all nations, from sea to sea, to the ends of the earth (v. 10). We haven't seen peace in all nations yet, but we will when Christ comes back.

Zechariah 9:11–17: Zechariah emphasized that when Jesus comes back to establish peace, He will release and restore His people. In this chapter, we see an incredible picture of God's judgment against everybody else and a deliverance and redemption of His people found only in the King who rides in on a donkey.

Zechariah 10:1–8: Over the course of time, the ten tribes had been lost and Judah had been scattered—all of them like sheep without a shepherd (v. 2). But "the cornerstone will come from Judah" (v. 4). And from those that have scattered, He will gather them back and they will fight. This seems to be a reference to both the first and second coming. The prophetic word always proclaims that Christ is the answer. God promised to strengthen, deliver, and restore the houses of Judah and Joseph "as though I had never rejected them" (v. 6). By God's grace and mercy, He gathers His people. The Cornerstone is Christ.

Zechariah 10:9–12: Again, though the people had been scattered through the nations, God promised to bring them back to the land. This chapter is all about God bringing His people back to the land.

Zechariah 11:1–6: In this chapter, you really begin to see Christ rejected by His people. In verses 1–6, we begin to see language about false shepherds. The false shepherds deceived people. J. Vernon McGee wondered if verse 6 might be a reference to Rome as the conqueror.[2]

Zechariah 11:7–14: The Shepherd used two staffs to shepherd the flock: favor and union (v. 7). The word "favor" could imply beauty or grace. The word "union" could imply a bond. Verses 12–13 are clearly about Judas' betrayal of Jesus. Matthew 26:15 said Judas was paid 30 pieces of silver for turning Jesus over to the chief priests. The same thing is written in Matthew 27:3–10 and Acts 1:17–20. This rejection of the King is recorded in Zechariah.

Notice the progression described in these three chapters. Zechariah 9 talked about the coming King. Zechariah 10 contained a reference to Christ as the Cornerstone. Now in Zechariah 11, Christ the King is rejected by His people. *Zechariah 11:15–17:* Who is the false shepherd in these verses? Possibly these verses are talking about the antichrist.

---

[2] McGee.

Zechariah 12:1–5: This chapter is the climax! Verse 1 provides a wonderful picture of the Lord's power. According to Wiersbe, verse 2 clearly spells out that Jerusalem will be attacked. In this instance, Jerusalem will be the cup that, when others attack her, they will start staggering. The nations will plan to swallow up Jerusalem, but as they're swallowing her up, it will lead to their staggering and demise.[3] Those who try to lift up Jerusalem will themselves be hurt (v. 3). In other words, God is clearly protecting Jerusalem—and it surely sounds like this happens "at the end." The phrase "on that day" found in verse 4 is language used to describe the Day of the Lord. When this battle takes place, God will create confusion, madness, and blindness for Jerusalem's enemies (v. 4). Wiersbe summarized: "Jesus Christ will demonstrate His great power as He defends His people and defeats His enemies."[4]

Zechariah 12:6–9: The siege against Jerusalem will also involve Judah. On that day, God will make Judah's leaders like a firepot and a flaming torch (v. 6). The power of God will be displayed through His people. Those who attack Judah will become like dry stubble that literally gets burned up. In fact, the Lord will save Judah first (v. 7). On that day, the Lord will defend Jerusalem (v. 8). Even the weakest one will be like David who killed tens of thousands (1 Samuel 18:7–8). The angel of the Lord killed 185,000 Assyrians in battle (Isaiah 37:36). All of their enemies will be destroyed. Verse 9 summarizes everything—God will destroy the nations that come against Jerusalem. In these verses, we've seen the Battle of Armageddon described.

Zechariah 12:10–14: Then, after the battle is won, God will pour out a spirit of grace and prayer on Jerusalem, and they will look at the One they pierced (v. 10). This is one of the most powerful statements in the Old Testament. Up until this point, the Jewish people have rejected Jesus. Now they will realize they crucified Jesus and will weep bitterly and mourn for Him. When this happens, a true revival like we've never seen in our lifetime will happen to usher in all that Christ has been talking about. The Jewish people realize they pierced the Messiah. Revelation 1:7 says everyone will see Christ when He returns, even those who pierced Him; they will mourn over Him. Paul wrote about this in Romans 11:25–27. Eventually, when all the Gentiles have heard the gospel, all of Israel will be saved. Somewhere in the Tribulation and the Day of the Lord, the fullness of the Gentiles will happen. At that point, God will open the eyes of the Jews and

---

[3] Warren W. Wiersbe, *The Wiersbe Bible Commentary: Old Testament* (Colorado Springs: David C. Cook, 2007), 1519.

[4] Wiersbe, 1519.

soften their hearts, and they will see they were the ones who pierced the Messiah. Then, they too, will turn to Christ as their Messiah.

Closing

Zechariah 12 points to one of the greatest moves of God still to come—when the Jewish people cry out to Yeshua.

The Daily Word

Zechariah proclaimed that one day the Jewish people will realize they pierced the Messiah. They will mourn and weep. They will know He is the One. They will grieve their disobedience and rejection of the Cornerstone, the Shepherd. They will lament piercing the heart of God. Yes, one day, Jesus will return on the clouds, and all will know He is the One they waited for.

Ask yourself: Have you acted like the Israelites, rejecting and walking in disobedience? Will you be surprised that Jesus is the Messiah? The Lord longs for you to wake up to His love, truth, and peace and receive Him into your life. Don't wait like the Israelites. Don't walk in your own ways and miss the Messiah right in front of you. Wake up and receive the truth. It's here for you. Yes, Jesus will come back. He wants you to know the truth so you may be set free and walk in peace. The Lord will never leave you. He loves you. Allow Him to be the cornerstone of your life, allow him to be your Great Shepherd, leading and guiding you. Allow Him to be your Messiah. Receive Him today.

Then, I will pour out a spirit of grace and prayer on the house of David and the residents of Jerusalem, and they will look at Me whom they pierced. They will mourn for Him as one mourns for an only child and weep bitterly for Him as one weeps for a firstborn. —Zechariah 12:10

Further Scripture: Zechariah 10:4; Romans 11:25–27; Revelation 1:7

Questions

1. Zechariah 9:9 says the King will ride on the colt of a donkey. Where in Scripture is this fulfilled (Mark 11:1–11)? Why would He ride the colt of a donkey and not a horse?

2. How would you explain Zechariah 10:2 to a new believer?

3. In Zechariah 10:6, God said He would restore Israel. In verses 8–9, God said He has redeemed them and they will return again to Israel. In your opinion, has this drawing back already started? Why or why not?

4. The people gave 30 pieces of silver for the worth of the Messiah in Zechariah 11:12. There are two other examples in Scripture where that amount is used (Exodus 21:32; Matthew 27:9). What are the differences between these? Why does Matthew attribute this quote to Jeremiah when it was clearly recorded by Zechariah?

5. In what ways does Zechariah 12:10 point to Jesus? Does this verse produce feelings of fear or triumph? How so?

6. What did the Holy Spirit highlight to you in Zechariah 9—12 through the reading or the teaching?

Lesson 21: Zechariah 13—14

Pierced One: Finding the Messiah in Zechariah

Teaching Notes

Intro

These chapters address Israel mourning the death of the One who was pierced. They also talk about the end of the age and how Jesus was the branch. In prophetic language, Zechariah may have been writing about the natural, current context, and then shift to what was supernatural. Arrogance and ignorance were frequently the attitudes of the people receiving the prophecy. The laws and the prophets all point to Jesus as the Messiah and His return. But the people did not understand. The Dutch Proverb, "Too soon old and too late smart," fit the mentality of the people.

Teaching

Zechariah 13:1–4: A time would come when the Jewish people would know exactly who Christ was. The Jews would be washed clean when they recognized who the Messiah was.

Cleansing of the land, prophets and unclean spirits would be removed is prophesied in verse 2. In Romans 11, Paul talked about the hardening of the heart of the Jewish people. But the time would come when the liberator would take away their sin.

In verse 3, the Lord of Host would erase the idols of the land. The idols were false and offered empty comfort. Idols offered something tangible that the people could see. Idols represented some kind of a reminder of the presence of God. People longed for what was lost. 2 Kings 18:3–4 state that Hezekiah destroyed the idols of the people of Israel. The people began to worship the things that brought the Israelites comfort and healing but they did not worship God. The people had remembered the moments of God's presence in their lives but they did not remember God.

In chapter 5, Zechariah talked about those that swear falsely being removed (vv. 1–4). These were the false prophets. The false prophets and the unclean would be removed.

Zechariah 13:5–8: Zechariah continued to announce the consequences of false prophets. The parents of the false prophets would remove them. These false prophets were trying to get a blessing, but not a blessing that came from God. In verse 5 God was erasing the false prophet issues.

Verse 6 and verse 7 are linked. Zechariah was talking about false prophets but switched to talking about the Messiah. In Verse 8, Zechariah proclaimed that two-thirds of the people would die but one-third would survive. This one-third represented the remnant that would survive. Zechariah explained that if the shepherd was removed, the sheep would scatter. These verses addressed the image of the people and the Messiah. The words of Christ in Mathew 26:3 talk about the disciples being scattered and were taken from Zechariah.

God preserved the remnant of Israel repeatedly. The references in Zechariah address the current context but also address what was to come at a time of judgment.

Zechariah 14:1–15: Zechariah began to address the tribulation time that was to come. God promised to avenge His people. God has compassion and mercy for His people. Zechariah stated that God would land on the Mount of Olives and split the mountain to create a valley. The people would flee by the mountain valley (vv. 1–5).

In Revelation 1:4–8, God promised that Christ would return and every eye would see Him. All the families of the earth would mourn for Him. These verses were taken from Zechariah. The Day of the Lord would come and it will be a day known only to Yahweh (vv. 6–7). In verse 8, Zechariah explained that water would flow from Jerusalem, half of it going to the Dead Sea and half of it going to the Mediterranean Sea. Yahweh would become king over all the earth. Ezekiel said that even the Dead Sea would become a place teaming with life.

Things would not be OK until Christ comes back. When Christ comes, things would be set right.

Closing

In Zechariah 14:16–21, the Scripture states that the nations would all worship God after a great battle takes place. The bottom line is that Christ would be the King, the Lord of Hosts. The people would go up to the Festival of Tabernacles. The words of "Holy to the Lord" would be even on the bells of the horses.

On that day, there would be no Canaanite in the house of the Lord. Everything would be as it should be when Christ comes again.

The Daily Word

As the prophet Zechariah concluded, he announced the Day of the Lord and the vision given to him—*Jesus will fight in battle,* and His feet will stand on the Mount of Olives facing Jerusalem to the east. The Mount of Olives will be split in half from east to west, forming a huge valley, so that half the mountain will move to the north and half will be south. When the Lord returns, there will no longer be impurity in His midst. Everyone will call upon the name of the Lord. Hallelujah! Jesus is returning. Wait for the Day of the Lord's return!

Behold, *the Lord reigns in your midst as a mighty warrior.* On the day of His return, He will fight for you because He loves you. He will be victorious. *Forever and ever, He will reign.* No longer will people be impure or hypocritical. No longer will there be idols or false worshippers. In the end, when Christ the Messiah returns, all will proclaim: "Our Lord and God—You are worthy to receive glory and honor and power because You have created all things, and because of Your will they exist and were created!" All the earth will see He is the Messiah. Prepare the way and go forth, proclaiming His name so all the world will know.

Then the Lord will go out to fight against those nations as He fights on a day of battle. —Zechariah 14:3

Further Scripture: Zechariah 14:11, 21; Revelation 4:11

Questions

1. In Zechariah 13:6, why would one ask, "What are these wounds in your hands?"

2. Do you believe Zechariah 13:8–9 as being literal? Does "parts" refer to objects or people? Why do you think that?

3. Zechariah 14:4 says the Mount of Olives will split and separate as a way of escape. Where else in Scripture did the Lord split something as a way of escape (Exodus 14:21–22)?

4. What did the Holy Spirit highlight to you in Zechariah 13—14 through the reading or the teaching?

Lesson 22: Malachi 1—4

Sun of Righteousness: Sun of Righteousness

Teaching Notes

Intro

The Old Testament was inspired by Matthew 5:17: "Don't assume that I came to destroy the Law or the Prophets. I did not come to destroy but to fulfill." Throughout the Minor Prophets, we've seen how Jesus came to fulfill the prophecies. Jesus has also been evident throughout the entire Old Testament.

Malachi is the last book of the Old Testament in both order and in historical chronology. God closed the canon of the Old Testament with His message through Malachi before a period of 400 years of His being quiet. Malachi's name means, "The Lord's Messenger." According to MacArthur, Jewish tradition placed Malachi in the Great Synagogue, a precursor to the Sanhedrin.[1]

Malachi prophesied in the late fifth century BC. Many scholars believe Malachi's ministry coincided with Nehemiah's return to Persia around 433–424 BC. Sacrifices were made at a physical temple during Malachi's ministry. Haggai and Zechariah had encouraged the people to finish building the temple. Malachi described offerings being made in this, the second temple, which was called Zerubbabel's temple (Malachi 1:7–11). The second temple was finished in 516 BC. In less than 100 years after the second temple was completed, MacArthur notes the priests had already become "complacent and corrupt."[2]

In addition to corrupting sacrifices, the Israelites were taking foreign wives, withholding tithes, and committing social injustice. It is almost as though the Israelites' history had reset after they returned from exile only for them to fall into the same pattern of sin and rebellion all over again. If Malachi did prophesy during Nehemiah's return to Persia, then the sins Nehemiah addressed on his return (Nehemiah 13:6) would be those described by Malachi.[3]

There would have been about 50,000 exiles who returned to Jerusalem from exile during Malachi's ministry. The temple had been rebuilt and the sacrificial

---

[1] John MacArthur, *The MacArthur Bible Commentary* (Nashville: Thomas Nelson, 2005), 1077.

[2] MacArthur, 1077–78.

[3] MacArthur, 1077–78.

system had been reinstated. But after a century of being back in the land, the people developed a hard-heartedness toward the Lord. Malachi rebuked the people and called them to repentance. As the Old Testament closed, MacArthur notes: "As over 2,000 years of Old Testament history takes place, since Abraham concluded, none of the glorious promises of the Abrahamic, Davidic, or the New Covenant have been fulfilled."[4] Malachi's primary prophecy was that the Messiah would not return until Israel repented of their sin.

Teaching

Malachi 1:1–5: Malachi opened with a picture of God's love for Israel (vv. 1–5). God pointed out how He chose Jacob over Esau. Even in Malachi's day, God's judgment on Edom, Esau's descendants, showed His care for Israel.

Malachi 1:6–14: God's complaint against His people included the priests. As God made His accusations, the people responded with sarcasm (vv. 6–7). The priests had robbed God of the honor due Him by bringing blind and lame animals to sacrifice to the Lord. In verse 8, the Lord challenged them to bring such offerings to their governor: "Would he be pleased with you or show you favor?" J. Vernon McGee pointed out that Israel's "hearts were polluted."[5] As a result, Israel should not expect to receive the Lord's favor. The Lord went so far as to say Israel should just shut the doors to the temple; He would "accept no offering from your hands" (v. 10), because God's people had misrepresented His name among the nations (v. 11). His people had backslidden to the extent that God had become boring to them.

Malachi 2: God warned the priests in regard to how they had led the people astray (vv. 1–7). The priests had turned away from God, so God pronounced that He had turned away from them (vv. 8–9).

Malachi 3:1–7: The "messenger" referred to in verse 1 would be John the Baptist. His role was to clear the way before Christ. Jesus quoted this passage in Matthew 11:10: "This is the one it is written about: Look, I am sending My messenger ahead of You; he will prepare Your way before you." After the messenger arrived, the Lord Himself promised to "suddenly come" (v. 1) at the temple. Part of the Lord's work would be to cleanse and purge the people and the priesthood. When He did that, Israel would present offerings that "will please the Lord as in the days of old and years gone by" (v. 4). This was a clear reference to the sacrifice of Jesus.

---

[4] MacArthur, 1077–78.

[5] J. Vernon McGee, *Malachi*, Thru the Bible Commentary Series (Nashville: Thomas Nelson, 1991), n. p.

Because God is a God who keeps His promises, He would ultimately deliver His people (v. 7).

Malachi 3:8–12: God also accused His people of robbing Him by not bringing their tithes (vv. 8–10). If God's people would give the way He commanded them to, God promised to bless them in such a way that "the nations will consider you fortunate" (v. 12). If not, God would judge them.

Malachi 3:13–18: God's people had further defamed Him by saying how "useless" it was to serve the Lord. As evidence, they sited how wicked people prospered (vv. 14–15). But there was a group that heard the accusations, "who feared the Lord and spoke to one another" (v. 16). God noticed their regard for Him and promised to "have compassion on them as a man has compassion on his son who serves him" (v. 17). The people would then see the true distinction between the righteous and the wicked by how God showed mercy to the repentant.

Malachi 4:1–4: The final chapter of Malachi began with a depiction of the Lord's day of judgment. God promised that "all the arrogant and everyone who commits wickedness" will be consumed (v. 1). But those who fear the Lord will "go out and playfully jump like calves from the stall" (v. 2). Malachi 4:2 is the verse from which our phrase from Malachi comes: *Sun of Righteousness.*

Malachi 4:5–6: Malachi closed with the promise of Elijah coming to the people before the day of His judgment. His job would be to "turn the hearts of fathers to their children and the hearts of children to their fathers" (v. 6). If he did not come, the Lord would curse the land.

Closing

Israel had two options. They could either continue to turn away from Him by offering contaminated offerings and turning away from their wives or they could be the faithful remnant that feared the Lord and looked forward to the coming of the *Sun of Righteousness.* Then God will pour out a blessing on them and restore families and your hearts and faith back to Him!

This concludes the Old Testament.

The Daily Word

The Lord heard the people say, "Look, what a nuisance," as they scorned His table. The people asked: "Have we wearied the Lord? How can we return? What have we spoken against you?" God's people were ignorant about how their words, actions, and heart condition affected the Lord. However, on the Day of the Lord, everyone will witness the arrogant and those who commit wickedness become stubble. But, *for those who fear God's name*, the sun of righteousness will rise with healing in its wings, and they will go out and playfully jump like calves from the stall.

Like the Israelites, God hears you when you mock Him. Yes, He sees you in your rebellion. Yes, He knows your thoughts. And He will consume you with fire if you do not turn back to Him. However, *for those who seek the Lord and fear Him, be prepared to dance and sing and play! The Day of the Lord will be upon us.* Stop arrogantly questioning God. Stop trying to figure out how far you can push it with Him. He sees you, He hears you, He knows you, and He wants your heart to be surrendered to Him. *That's it.* Then you will have joy, peace, and salvation. Jesus will be enough, and this truth will set you free to playfully jump like a calf!

"But for you who fear My name, the sun of righteousness will rise with healing in its wings, and you will go out and playfully jump like calves from the stall. You will trample the wicked, for they will be ashes under the soles of your feet on the day I am preparing," says the Lord of Hosts. —Malachi 4:2–3

Further Scripture: Psalm 16:11; 73:25–28; Malachi 1:13; 3:13–14

Questions

1. Did Malachi 1:11 predict the gospel going out to the Gentiles in Acts 10?

2. What issues did the Lord say He had with the offerings that were given to Him in Malachi 1?

3. The Lord said that He "hates divorce" (Malachi 2:16). Did God ever give permission for divorce? If so, in what instances (Matthew 5:32; 1 Corinthians 7:12–16)?

4. The Lord commanded His people to tithe to the "storehouse" in Malachi 3:10. In Malachi's day, the storehouse would have been the temple. Today, the storehouse is where your soul is being fed. Do you tithe? Why or why not? Has there been a time that you knew the Lord was "rebuking the devourer for your sakes" (Malachi 3:11)?

5. In Malachi 4:5, the Lord said Elijah the Prophet would be sent. Where else in Scripture was the coming of Elijah mentioned (Matthew 17:10–12; Revelation 11:3)?

6. What did the Holy Spirit highlight to you in Malachi 1—4 through the reading or the teaching?

Contributing Authors

Dr. Kyle Lance Martin
Kyle Lance Martin is the founder of Time to Revive, a ministry based in Dallas, Texas, whose mission is to equip the saints for the return of Christ. His heart's desire, aside from loving his wife and four kids, is to engage people with the Word of God directly in their own environment. Kyle believes when people turn to the Messiah in humility and have a willingness to walk in the Holy Spirit, they can know and experience the calling of being a disciple of Jesus Christ. Kyle received his master of biblical studies from Dallas Theological Seminary and his doctor of ministry in outreach and discipleship from Gordon-Conwell Theological Seminary.

Pastor Gordon Henke
Gordon Henke is a pastor from northern Indiana, serving the church for 25 years. His passion is the studying of the Word. With confidence in the truth of the Word, he passionately helps people boldly share their faith.

Pastor Tom Schiefer
Tom Schiefer is the senior pastor of Nappanee First Brethren Church in Nappanee, Indiana. Prior to accepting a call to pastoral ministry, he was a band and choir director in Ohio. In the context of these two careers, he loves to orchestrate the Word of God, and the message it contains, into harmony with people's lives.

Pastor Fred Stayton
Fred Stayton is the lead pastor of Sonrise Church in Fort Wayne, Indiana, and has a passion for turning the hearts of fathers back to their children. Fred and his wife, Cheryl, have six children and one grandchild.

Ryan Schrag
Ryan Schrag is the national director for Time to Revive and has a heart to "equip the saints for the return of Christ" in the United States. Prior to joining full-time ministry, he was formerly the owner/operator of a lawn care business.

Wesley Morris
Wesley Morris is the Georgia state chairman for Time to Revive. A former construction worker turned pastor, he now trains and equips people to encounter Jesus and boldly share their faith.

Josh Edwards

Josh Edwards is the Minnesota state chairman for Time to Revive and leads worship both nationally and internationally. For the past 20 years he has been leading worship and speaking to the body of Christ about his heart's desire to see the church united, revived, and equipped to do the work of the ministry.

Shawn Carlson

Shawn Carlson is the executive director for Time to Revive. He has a strong desire to see people grow closer to Jesus through the study of God's Word and the carrying out of His mission.

Matt Reynolds

Matt Reynolds is the president of Spirit & Truth, a ministry aimed at equipping believers and churches to be more empowered by the Spirit, rooted in the truth, and mobilized for the mission. After serving as a local pastor for 13 years, Matt responded to a missionary calling to pursue Spirit-filled renewal in the church.

Larry Hopkins

Larry Hopkins is a businessman and entrepreneur in Dallas, Texas, who loves studying and discussing God's Word. He has a heart for revival, which stems from his love and desire for the Bible.

Pastor Kyle Felke

Kyle Felke is a former pastor in northern Indiana. He grew up in a home where both parents were teachers, which instilled in him a passion for teaching. This, combined with a love for Jesus, led him to pursue a biblical education and pastor a church in northern Indiana.

Contributing Authors

The Pentateuch
Kyle Lance Martin

The Gospels
Kyle Lance Martin
Josh Edwards
Ryan Schrag
Matt Reynolds

The Historical Books
Kyle Lance Martin
Wesley Morris
Josh Edwards
Pastor Gordon Henke
Pastor Tom Schiefer
Pastor Kyle Felke
Larry Hopkins

Acts
Kyle Lance Martin
Pastor Gordon Henke
Pastor Tom Schiefer
Wesley Morris
Shawn Carlson

The Wisdom Books
Kyle Lance Martin
Pastor Gordon Henke
Pastor Tom Schiefer
Wesley Morris
Ryan Schrag
Pastor Fred Stayton
Shawn Carlson
Josh Edwards

Paul's Letters
Kyle Lance Martin
Pastor Gordon Henke
Pastor Tom Schiefer
Wesley Morris
Shawn Carlson
Josh Edwards
Ryan Schrag

The Major Prophets
Kyle Lance Martin
Pastor Gordon Henke
Pastor Tom Schiefer
Pastor Fred Stayton
Ryan Schrag
Josh Edwards

General Letters
Kyle Lance Martin
Pastor Fred Stayton
Shawn Carlson

The Minor Prophets
Kyle Lance Martin
Josh Edwards

Revelation
Kyle Lance Martin
Pastor Gordon Henke
Pastor Tom Schiefer

www.ingramcontent.com/pod-product-compliance
Lightning Source LLC
Chambersburg PA
CBHW060813100426
42813CB00004B/1058